T0128537

THE CIA'S GREATEST HITS

FULLY REVISED AND UPDATED

SECOND EDITION

MARK ZEPEZAUER

THE REAL STORY SERIES

PUBLISHED BY SOFT SKULL PRESS

THIS BOOK IS DEDICATED TO
FORREST LLOYD ZEPEZAUER,
A KEEN STUDENT OF HISTORY.

Research, writing and illustrations: **Mark Zepezauer**

Editing, design and layout: **Arthur Naiman**

Copyediting and proofreading:
   Susan McCallister, John Kadyk, Arthur Naiman

Index: **Ty Koontz, Arthur Naiman**

Title: **Charlie Winton**

Series editor: **Arthur Naiman**

Fonts: **Bookman** *(text and chapter titles)*

   Optima *(table of contents, sources, index*
       and notes like these)

   LIBERTY *(headers and footers, heads on p. 112)*

   LITHOS *(front cover, title page, dedication, etc.)*

   Gill Sans *(copy on back cover and on p. 112)*

Printed in the USA   ISBN: 978-1-59376-439-5

THE REAL STORY SERIES
IS PUBLISHED BY SOFT SKULL PRESS AND
DISTRIBUTED BY PUBLISHERS GROUP WEST

Introduction

In order to survive, nations need effective intelligence services. But the idea that the CIA is primarily an information-gathering operation is itself one of the agency's greatest propaganda triumphs. Despite its name, the Central Intelligence Agency's main purpose has always been to carry out covert operations that involve everything from rigged elections, economic warfare and drug trafficking to torture, assassinations, bombings, wars and even genocide.

The CIA also spends a lot of time distorting intelligence, and this "disinformation" has led to dangerous illusions among our policymakers and the public. (It also works the other way around, of course, as when George W. Bush's administration custom-ordered the "evidence" it needed to justify its invasion of Iraq.)

But covert operations, not information-gathering (or disinformation-dispensing), are the lifeblood of the CIA. Its main purpose has always been to provide "plausible deniability" to the government—it does the dirty deeds the government wants done but doesn't want to admit to. And if, despite its best efforts, these secret crimes are discovered, out comes the all-purpose shroud of "national security."

Many people think of the CIA as a rogue agency but Noam Chomsky disagrees: "The CIA is very much under the control of executive power. . . . It's very rare for [it] to undertake initiatives on its own. It often looks as though it does, but that's because the executive wants to preserve deniability." (For a couple of possible exceptions to this general rule, see pp. 24–25 and 52–53.)

This book provides concise descriptions of forty-eight of the CIA's most heinous crimes—and that's *far* from a complete list. For more details about each of them, see the *Sources* section that begins on page 104. I've also provided a more extensive list of sources online at *http://tinyurl.com/CIAsources,* along with a glossary of important terms and names.

After the first edition of this book came out, I received some criticism that it was an attack on the hardworking men and women of the CIA (who included, as it happens, my late father-in-law). To that I say: It's never the people caught in a system who deserve the lion's share of the blame, but the system itself.

And that system, using "national security" as its pretext, has made us all much less secure. It's spawned new and impassioned enemies who threaten our safety and well-being. It's brought dishonor to our country and to what we claim to stand for.

To demand that we live up to the standards we espouse is not an attack on the American way of life—it's a duty for anyone who believes in those standards and that way of life.

The abominations described in this book are enough to chill the bones of anybody who cares about liberty and justice. If those are more than just words to you, we hope you'll join us in working to end the CIA's long, ugly subversion of our democracy.

Mark Zepezauer

About Mark Zepezauer

Mark Zepezauer was raised amid the idyllic semiconductor farms of Silicon Valley, the son of immigrants from Milwaukee and Chicago. After graduating from the Santa Cruz campus of the University of California, he worked for several Santa Cruz newspapers and created the cartoon series *US History Backwards*, which tells the story of the country beginning in the present and working back in time.

In 1989 he produced a limited edition art book, *The Nixon Saga*, which was purchased by two museums. In 1993 he moved to Arizona and began publishing the *Tucson Comic News*, a monthly compendium of political cartoons and commentary that lasted for seven years.

Zepezauer wrote the first edition of this book in 1994. He's also the author of *Take the Rich Off Welfare* (1996; second edition, 2004) and *Boomerang! How Our Covert Wars Have Created Enemies Across the Middle East and Brought Terror to America* (2003).

He lives in Tucson with his splendid wife, two miraculous children, a goofball dog and two recalcitrant cats. He blogs sporadically at *www.markzepezauer.com*.

Contents

Hit #1: *How the Nazis Won the War*

One of the most important of all CIA operations began before the agency was even born. Long before World War II ended, many Nazi leaders realized they were going to lose, so they started negotiating with the US behind Hitler's back about a possible future war against the USSR. In 1943, future CIA Director Allen Dulles moved to Bern, Switzerland, to begin back-channel talks with these influential Nazis.

Officially, Dulles was an agent of the OSS (the Office of Strategic Services, the CIA's predecessor) but he wasn't above pursuing his own agenda with the Nazis, many of whom he had worked with before the war. Indeed, as a prominent Wall Street lawyer, Dulles had a number of clients—Standard Oil, for one—who continued doing business with the Nazis *during* the war.

So it's not surprising that when Hitler's intelligence chief for the Eastern front, General Reinhard Gehlen (GAY-len), surrendered to the US, he expected a warm reception—especially since he had buried his extensive files in a secret spot and planned to use them as a negotiating chip.

General Gehlen was whisked to Fort Hunt, Virginia, where he soon succeeded in convincing his captors that the Soviet Union was about to attack the West. The US Army and Gehlen arrived at a "gentlemen's agreement."

According to the secret treaty, his spy organization (which came to be called the Gehlen Org) would work for—and be funded by—the US until a new German government came to power. In the meantime, should Gehlen find a conflict between German interests and US ones, he was free to consider the German ones

8

first. Gehlen even made sure to get approval for this arrangement from Hitler's appointed successor, Admiral Doenitz, who was in a cushy prisoner-of-war camp for Nazi VIPs in Wiesbaden, Germany.

For almost ten years, the Gehlen Org was virtually the CIA's only source of intelligence on Eastern Europe. Then, in 1955, it evolved into the BND (the German equivalent of the CIA)—which, of course, continued to cooperate with the CIA.

Gehlen was far from the only Nazi war criminal employed by the CIA. Others included Klaus Barbie ("the Butcher of Lyon"), Otto von Bolschwing (the Holocaust mastermind who worked closely with Eichmann) and SS Colonel Otto Skorzeny (a great favorite of Hitler's). There's even evidence that Martin Bormann, Hitler's second-in-command at the end of the war, faked his own death and escaped to Latin America, where he worked with CIA-linked groups.

Hit #2: *Operation Gladio*

The CIA was created by the National Security Act of 1947. The ink was barely dry on it before an army of spooks began marching through the law's major loophole: the CIA could "perform such other functions and duties . . . as the National Security Council may from time to time direct." This deliberately vague clause opened the door to more than sixty years of criminal activity in the name of "national security."

One of the first duties the NSC deemed necessary was the subversion of Italian democracy . . . in the name of democracy, of course. Italy seemed likely to elect a leftist government in the 1948 election. To make sure Italians voted instead for the candidates Washington favored—leftover blackshirt thugs from Mussolini's fascist party and other Nazi collaborators—millions of dollars were spent on propaganda and payoffs. It was also intimated that food aid would be cut off if the election results were inconsistent with US desires.

The US got its way in 1948 without having to resort to violence but—as was discovered in 1990—the CIA had organized a secret paramilitary army in postwar Italy, with hidden stockpiles of weapons and explosives dotting the map. Called Operation Gladio (from the Latin *gladius*, a type of short sword), the ostensible excuse for it was laughable—the threat of a Soviet invasion. But the real purpose wasn't so funny—Operation Gladio's 15,000 troops were trained to overthrow the Italian government should it stray from the straight and narrow.

Similar secret armies were formed in France, Belgium, the Netherlands and West Germany—often directed, quite naturally, by former SS officers. They didn't just wait around for the Russians to come marching in; they assembled huge arms caches (many of which remain unaccounted for), compiled blacklists of leftists and, in France, participated in plots to assassinate President De Gaulle.

Many members of Operation Gladio were also in a shadowy organization known as P-2; it too was financed by the CIA. P-2 had connections with the Vatican and the Mafia, and eventually with an international fascist umbrella organization called the World Anti-Communist League (see Hit #32).

One of P-2's specialties was the art of provocation. Leftist organizations like the Red Brigades were infiltrated, financed and/or created, and the resulting acts of terrorism, like the assassination of Italy's premier in 1978 and the bombing of the railway station in Bologna in 1980, were blamed on the left. The goal of this "strategy of tension" was to convince Italian voters that the left was violent and dangerous—by helping make it so.

Hit #3: **Destroying Iranian Democracy**

The history of the CIA in Iran shows that it isn't the failures of the agency we need to worry about, numerous though they are. Its successes—and Iran is one of the biggest—are far more dangerous.

The CIA did exactly what was asked of it in Iran, deposing of a mildly nationalist regime that was a minor irritant to US policymakers. As a direct result, a fiercely nationalist regime came to power 26 years later, and it's proved to be a major irritant to the US ever since.

In 1951, Dr. Mohammad Mossadegh, "the most popular politician in the country," was elected prime minister of Iran. His major election plank was the nationalization of the only oil company operating in Iran at that time—British Petroleum. The nationalization bill was passed unanimously by the Iranian parliament.

Though Mossadegh offered BP considerable compensation, his days were numbered from that point on. The British coordinated an international economic embargo of Iran, throwing its economy into chaos. And the CIA, at the request of the British, began spending millions of dollars on ways to get rid of Mossadegh.

The CIA's plans hinged on the young Shah of Iran, Reza Pahlavi, a timid and inexperienced figurehead. (He was a mere shadow of his father, who had led a pro-Nazi regime during World War II.) In 1953, with CIA backing, the Shah ordered Mossadegh out of office and appointed a Nazi collaborator as his successor. Demonstrators filled the streets in support of Mossadegh, and the Shah fled to Rome.

Undaunted, the CIA paid for pro-Shah street demonstrators, who seized a radio station and announced that the Shah was on his way back and that Mossadegh had been deposed. In reality, it took a nine-hour tank battle in the streets of Tehran, killing hundreds, to remove Mossadegh.

Compared to the bloodshed to follow, however, that was just a drop in the bucket. In 1976, Amnesty International concluded that the Shah's CIA-trained security force, SAVAK, had the worst human rights record on the planet, and that the number and variety of torture techniques the CIA had taught SAVAK were "beyond belief."

Inevitably, in 1979, the Iranian people over-threw the bloodstained Shah, with great bitter-ness and hatred toward the US for installing him and backing him all those years. The radi-cal fundamentalist regime that rules Iran today could never have found popular support with-out the CIA's 1953 coup and the repression that followed.

Hit #4:

Destroying Guatemalan Democracy

If you ever need a reminder that the CIA was founded and run by lawyers, you won't need to look any further than the overthrow of Guatemalan democracy. The Dulles brothers were partners in the Wall Street law firm of Sullivan & Cromwell; time permitting, they also worked for the US government. With John Foster Dulles heading the State Department and Allen Dulles heading the CIA, they were the czars of Eisenhower's foreign policy, and they made sure that the interests of Sullivan & Cromwell clients weren't ignored.

In 1951, Jacobo Arbenz was elected president of Guatemala by a landslide in a free and fair election. He hoped to transform Guatemala "from a backward country with a predominantly feudal economy to a modern capitalist state." The CIA, however, weighed in heavily on the side of feudalism.

When Arbenz appropriated some unused land controlled by the Rockefeller-owned United Fruit Company (for which United Fruit was fairly compensated), the company undertook an extensive PR campaign in the US, designed to paint Arbenz as a tool of the "international Communist conspiracy." John Foster Dulles, ever alert for opportunities to roll back the red menace—and to help out a valued client—convinced Ike that Arbenz must go.

Brother Allen's CIA was only too happy to take on the job, which ended up costing only about $20 million. The agency sponsored a propaganda offensive and hired about 300 mercenaries who sporadically sabotaged trains and oil supplies.

Finally, in June of 1954, unmarked CIA planes staged a series of air raids on the Guatemalan capital and dropped leaflets demanding Arbenz's resignation. At the same time, CIA-run radio stations warned of the impending invasion of an occupying rebel army (actually the agency's 300 hired thugs). Considering discretion the better part of valor, Arbenz fled, leaving Guatemala in the hands of the CIA's hand-picked stooge, General Carlos Castillo Armas.

The CIA has always been particularly proud of the Guatemalan operation, which inaugurated a series of bloodthirsty regimes that murdered more than 100,000 Guatemalans. In retrospect, however, some CIA veterans concluded that it may have come off too easily, leading to a certain overconfidence. As one CIA officer put it, "We thought we could knock off these little brown people on the cheap."

Hit #5: *Mind Control Experiments*

The CIA says its mind control experiments were a strictly defensive response to Chinese "brainwashing" of US POWs during the Korean War (captured US pilots were making public statements denouncing US germ warfare against civilians). Actually, US brainwashing experiments predate the CIA itself.

CIA mind control activities (also called *behavior control*) did accelerate in 1953, under a program that was exempt from the usual oversight procedures. Code-named MK-ULTRA, many of its files were destroyed by CIA Director Richard Helms (who was with it from the start) when he left office in 1973, but the surviving history is nasty enough.

MK-ULTRA spooks and shrinks tested radiation, electric shocks, electrode implants, microwaves, ultrasound and a wide range of drugs on unwitting subjects, including hundreds of prisoners at California's infamous Vacaville State Prison.

The CIA saw mind control as a way to create torture-proof couriers (by implanting memories that can only be retrieved with a prearranged signal) and programmed assassins, as in *The Manchurian Candidate.* There's evidence that Sirhan Sirhan was treated by a CIA-linked shrink before killing RFK (see Hit #16).

The agency also wondered if it could disorient its adversaries with mind-altering substances like LSD. It was so fascinated with LSD that, in 1953, it tried to buy up the entire world supply. For many years, the agency was the principal source of LSD in the US, both legal and otherwise (one CIA-connected dealer produced tens of millions of doses).

Before ultimately dismissing LSD as unpredictable, the CIA tested it on countless people—including its own—without their consent, provoking several suicides. One CIA germ-warfare expert hurled himself out of a tenth-story window—or was pushed—after a "surprise" dose. It was 22 years before his family found out the real reason for his death.

The agency also rented a series of apartments, staffed them with prostitutes and watched through one-way mirrors to see the effects of various substances the prostitutes slipped to the unlucky johns. When CIA auditors found out about this (in 1963), MK-ULTRA was supposedly shut down. In fact, it was simply renamed MKSEARCH, and some of its more exotic projects were trimmed.

The CIA says all its behavior control operations ended when Helms left in 1973. If you believe that, maybe they *did* learn some useful techniques from all those brainwashing experiments. (Also see Hit #28.)

Hit #6: *Bloodbaths in the Congo*

When Congo (called Zaire from 1971 to 1997) won its independence from Belgium in 1960, Patrice Lumumba became its first prime minister. He was a charismatic leader who enjoyed strong support in the parliament, but he was able to hold office for only two months.

A leftist, Lumumba attempted to steer a neutral course between the US and the USSR—no easy task. As Kwame Nkrumah of Ghana observed, it was perfectly all right for Britain and France to maintain diplomatic relations with the Soviet Union, but any African leader who dared do this became an enemy of the US.

Such was the fate of Lumumba. Though the CIA "regularly bought and sold Congolese politicians," it feared that Lumumba's oratorical talents would make him a thorn in their side, even if he were maneuvered out of power. So they decided it would be safer to kill him.

CIA Director Allen Dulles ordered Lumumba's assassination. (A 1975 Congressional inquiry decided that "a reasonable inference" could be drawn that this was done with Eisenhower's assent.) The agency dispatched a lethal virus to Africa, but before it could be used on Lumumba, he was deposed by Congo's CIA-backed president and fled for his life.

With the CIA's help, Lumumba was captured in December 1960 by the troops of General Joseph Mobutu, who'd assumed control of the government. Lumumba was held prisoner for over a month, interrogated, tortured, then finally shot in the head. His body was dissolved in hydrochloric acid.

Mobutu ran Congo for nearly forty years, and the lure of the country's vast mineral resources led the CIA into a marriage of convenience with him. (The CIA station in Congo was the largest in Africa.)

Almost 40% of Congo's revenues flowed to him and his cronies. While the average Congolese made $190 a year, Mobutu became a billionaire.

He handed out life sentences to student protesters for "insulting the president," tossed opposition politicians into mental hospitals, suppressed religion and the press. He was so hated by his countrymen that he only felt safe living on a barge in the middle of the Congo River.

Eventually, Mobutu's cruelty alarmed even the CIA, who supported a 1977 uprising against him. But when it failed, the CIA and Mobutu kissed and made up. He was finally deposed in 1997 and died in exile, but the evil he did lives on: Congo has been wracked with warfare ever since his corrupt, brutal rule.

Hit #7: *The U-2 Incident*

Toward the end of his career, President Eisenhower began to have second thoughts about the people he'd served faithfully all his life. In his farewell address to the nation, he warned of "the potential for the disastrous rise of misplaced power" inherent in the "military-industrial complex."

At least some of Ike's misgivings could be traced to the U-2 incident that happened eight months earlier. He'd planned a peace summit involving the leaders of the US, the USSR, Britain and France. It was to be the culmination of his "crusade for peace" and a limited nuclear test ban treaty was supposed to emerge from it.

Then, on the eve of the conference, an American U-2 spy plane landed smack in the middle of Russia. Worse, the Eisenhower administration was caught in a lie. First it claimed that an "unarmed weather research flight" had strayed into Soviet territory. Then it learned that the pilot, Francis Gary Powers, had been captured alive, thousands of miles from any border—and on May Day, no less. The Soviets were predictably incensed, and the summit was called off.

In fact, contrary to Soviet claims and press reports, the U-2 wasn't shot down—it descended and crash-landed due to a fuel shortage. This was revealed by CIA Director Allen Dulles at a secret congressional hearing (the record of which was declassified in 1975).

At the same hearing, Dulles casually remarked that he "assumed" the U-2 flight had been authorized by the president. This was highly unlikely (to say the least) since Ike had not only ordered that all such flights be curtailed in preparation for his historic summit with Khrushchev, but he'd also temporarily scaled back covert operations in Cuba and Tibet as a way of showing good faith.

It's much more likely that the crash of the U-2 was intended to sabotage the peace summit. In addition to fearing a lessening of tensions with the Soviet Union, US hard-liners were incensed at Ike's failure to back the CIA-inspired Hungarian uprising in 1956 (although if he had, it could have led to nuclear war).

Ike took full responsibility for the U-2 incident—it was either that or admit it had been done behind his back. But in a taped phone call to John McCone (who became JFK's CIA director), Ike—working on his memoirs—groped for an explanation: "I don't want to be accusing people of having fooled me, but . . . . "

Hit #8: *The Bay of Pigs Invasion*

When Cuban revolutionary Fidel Castro over-threw the US-backed Batista dictatorship in 1959, he closed down the casinos and brothels and nationalized all businesses. This deprived the Mafia—and other US-based multinationals—of a very profitable cash cow.

Vice President Richard Nixon, who had long-standing ties with the Mob (through his best friend, Bebe Rebozo, among others), began plotting with the CIA to eliminate Castro. They did this largely behind Eisenhower's back, fully expecting that Nixon would be the next president. When JFK was elected instead, he inherited an operation—an invasion of Cuba at the Bay of Pigs—about which he had serious misgivings.

While JFK was eager to get rid of Castro, he didn't want to use US forces to do it—just Cuban exiles. The CIA hoped they could provoke an incident that would force JFK to use the US military. When he held his ground and refused, the whole invasion failed (in April 1961).

It probably wouldn't have succeeded in any case. Security for the operation was poor, as was the training given to the 1500-man invasion force. A planned phony attack on the US base at Guantanamo never happened, nor did the agency's other ace in the hole—the assassination of Castro.

The CIA had hired the Mafia to kill Castro (something they both dearly desired); the hit was to occur at the same time as the invasion. Ironically, because the CIA's left hand didn't know what its right hand was doing, the Mob's hit man was almost assassinated himself. He was one of eight JFK-backed exile leaders chosen to head a post-Castro government, but Nixon had them detained during the invasion. If the invasion had succeeded, all eight would have been killed, so that Nixon-backed Cubans could take over.

To shift blame from themselves, and to embarrass JFK into more militant actions, the CIA mounted a propaganda campaign that attributed the whole Bay of Pigs failure to JFK's decision to cancel a crucial air strike. In fact, the decision had been made behind JFK's back—though he took full responsibility for it, as President Eisenhower did in a similar situation (see Hit #7).

After JFK's death, the CIA's war against Castro continued. The agency tried to kill Castro more than two dozen times, up until at least 1987. There have also been numerous cases of CIA sabotage in Cuba, including the use of germ warfare.

As for the Cuban exiles involved in the Bay of Pigs, many have turned to organized crime and freelance terrorism (see Hit #26 for an example). Others have continued to work for the CIA on covert operations. And many, of course, do both.

Hit #9: *The JFK Assassination*

If the CIA had nothing to do with the assassination of President John F. Kennedy, they certainly have a peculiar way of showing it, since they've undermined every investigation into his murder. This is hardly surprising, given the disproportionate number of CIA connections to the case.

Take the accused "lone nut," Lee Harvey Oswald. As a Marine, he was stationed at Atsugi Air Base in Japan, one of the largest CIA stations in the world and home of the ultra-secret U-2 spy plane (see Hit #7).

Before his transparently phony "defection" to the USSR in 1959, Oswald studied Russian in the military. In Moscow, he renounced his citizenship to a CIA officer at the US Embassy, promising to tell the Russians all he knew about the U-2. When he "changed his mind" two years later, the State Department cheerfully returned his passport and loaned him the money for his trip home.

Oswald was met in New York by a member of a CIA front group that was full of Nazis. He then moved to Dallas, where he was "befriended" by Count George de Mohrenschildt, who admitted shortly before his death that he'd been assigned by the CIA to debrief Oswald on his Russian sojourn.

When Oswald moved to New Orleans in the summer of 1963, he became involved, wittingly or unwittingly, with three far-right agents of the CIA who were conspiring to assassinate JFK, ostensibly for his "betrayal" at the Bay of Pigs (see Hit #8)—Guy Banister, with whom Oswald worked while continuing to pose as a Marxist; Clay Shaw, who would later be acquitted of involvement in the JFK assassination at a trial where the prosecution tried but failed to obtain proof of his CIA status; and David Ferrie, whose Civil Air Patrol unit Oswald had joined when he was fifteen.

Back in Dallas that fall, Oswald was seen in the company of one "Maurice Bishop," later identified as David Atlee Phillips, who was part of a group of CIA officers that despised JFK. It included the fanatical William Harvey (who had strong links to the Mafia—he hired Johnny Rosselli to have Castro killed) and future Watergate burglar Howard Hunt, who would later lose a libel suit against a newspaper that said he was involved in the JFK assassination.

There are several possible motives for CIA involvement in the assassination: JFK's perceived "softness" on Communism, the fact that he'd fired CIA Director Allen Dulles and Deputy Director Charles Cabell (brother of the mayor of Dallas), and a statement he made shortly after the Bay of Pigs in which he promised to "splinter the CIA into a thousand pieces and scatter it to the winds."

Hit #10: *Vietnam 1945–63*

Long before the US military got involved there directly, Vietnam was the CIA's war. At first they collaborated with the French, who struggled for nine years, from 1945 to 1954, to recapture their one-time colony (despite the war's unpopularity with the French public).

Even with CIA mercenaries fighting alongside the French, and air support from the CIA's Air America (at the time, the largest "private" airline in the world), the effort proved to be in vain.

The 1954 Geneva Accords temporarily divided Vietnam in preparation for elections in 1956. But the US wasn't interested in elections.

In the North, CIA "psywar" expert Ed Lansdale spread the rumor that the US was planning to nuke the area. This—along with other, similar tactics—created an exodus of over one million refugees, who were ferried to the south by CIA ships and planes.

In the South, the CIA wrote a constitution for "South Vietnam" (which had never been considered a separate country before), installed Ngo Dinh Diem and gave him the job of crushing anyone who had opposed the French.

US support for Diem was based on the belief that he was the one politician in Vietnam who would never negotiate with Ho Chi Minh. When, after nine more years of futile warfare, even Diem decided that negotiations would be desirable, he was tossed aside as casually as he'd been put in place. In November 1963, he was deposed in a CIA-sponsored coup, then assassinated.

In 1945, a US intelligence agent described Ho Chi Minh as the "strongest and perhaps the ablest figure in Indochina, and . . . any suggested solution which excludes him is . . . of uncertain outcome." Unfortunately, such insights were ignored in Washington as the Cold War solidified.

Hit #11:
Destroying Dominican Democracy

Rafael Trujillo took power in the Dominican Republic in a 1930 *coup d'état* and received enthusiastic backing from Washington for most of the next thirty years. His methods for suppressing dissent were sickeningly familiar: torture and mass murder. The US raised no objections, and Trujillo returned the favor by becoming a totally reliable supporter of US policies in the UN.

As often happens with such tyrants, however, he got too greedy. His personal business holdings grew until he controlled some three-fifths of the Dominican economy, which threatened the "favorable investment climate" that client states are set up for in the first place.

Also, when it started to look like Castro's revolutionary army would take over Cuba, the US began to worry that Trujillo's excesses might inspire a similar revolution in the Dominican Republic. Whatever the reasons, the CIA began plotting Trujillo's assassination in 1958.

His life came to an abrupt end in May 1961, and while plausible deniability was maintained in Washington, this is one of the best-documented CIA assassination plots (according to the 1975 Church Committee). The US attempted to maintain the corrupt essence of the Trujillo regime without Trujillo, but the 1962 elections brought a physician named Juan Bosch to power.

Bosch was anti-Communist and pro-business but—foolish man—he was dedicated to establishing a "decent democratic regime" through land reform, low-rent housing and public works projects. He was deposed by a CIA-backed coup after only seven months in office. When a popular countercoup tried to restore Bosch to power in 1965, the US invaded the island and installed a series of murderous regimes which have maintained a "favorable investment climate" ever since.

While he never lived long enough to see it enshrined as the "JFK Doctrine," President Kennedy once offered a fairly clear-cut rationale for US interventions abroad. Referring to the Dominican Republic, he said, "There are three possibilities . . . a decent democratic regime, a continuation of the Trujillo regime, or a Castro regime [by which he meant Bosch]. We ought to aim at the first, but we really can't renounce the second until we are sure that we can avoid the third."

In practice, we've hardly ever used the first option. Virtually all of our Cold War clients were murderous dictatorships like the Trujillo regime (and like the regimes we replaced him with).

Hit #12: *The Malcolm X Assassination*

In the last years of his life, Malcolm X did a number of things that angered the CIA. For example, he stated many times that he believed the CIA was behind the Lumumba assassination (it was—see Hit #6). He held widely publicized meetings with anti-imperialist Third World leaders, many of whom were later overthrown or killed in CIA-backed operations. And he planned to ask the UN to officially declare American blacks an "oppressed minority," which would have been a major embarrassment to the US. (Ten years earlier, the CIA had ruined the career of black leader Paul Robeson over the same threat.)

But another development scared the government even more: No longer a separatist (he split from the Nation of Islam a year before his death),

Malcolm was forging alliances with more moderate black leaders. If he'd lived just a week longer, he would have had his first cooperative meeting with Martin Luther King. Soon after that, he would have gone to Algeria for a summit meeting of nonwhite resistance movements from all over the world.

In a coordinated effort, the FBI and the CIA had been spying on Malcolm for years, and both the Nation of Islam and Malcolm's splinter group, the OAAU, were heavily infiltrated by government agents. In fact, one of Malcolm's bodyguards on the night he was slain was working for the New York Police Department's intelligence unit; he left the scene shortly before the shooting started.

Malcolm expressed doubts to his biographer that the Nation of Islam could be behind all the things that had happened to him in the year before he was killed. "I know what they can do and what they can't do," he'd said, "and they can't do some of the stuff recently going on."

In February 1965, while giving a speech in Harlem, Malcolm was shot to death by five gunmen. All but one of the assassins escaped. The three men eventually charged with the murder were all members of the Nation of Islam. In 1979, one of them revealed that the conspiracy to kill Malcolm had included one of the highest-ranking FBI infiltrators in the organization.

With Malcolm dead, the coalition between the more radical and the more moderate wings of the black liberation movement never came to pass. His resolution regarding the oppression of American blacks did reach the floor of the UN, but without Malcolm's charisma to draw attention to it, it was ignored.

Hit #13: *Bloodbath in Indonesia*

Some people justify the CIA's crimes by saying that we faced a brutal and ruthless enemy in the Cold War, and winning was of paramount importance. The problem with that argument is that no one could have been more brutal and ruthless than the allies we embraced. There's no clearer illustration of this than Indonesia, the fourth most populous nation on Earth.

From 1945 to 1965, the president of Indonesia was Sukarno. A star among Third World leaders, active in the nonaligned, anti-imperialist movement, he'd long been a thorn in the side of the US. Even worse, the Communist party was part of his governing coalition. The CIA had backed a failed uprising against him in 1958, had tried to assassinate him, and had even attempted to embarrass him by making a porno film starring a Sukarno look-alike!

In 1965, they finally scored. The Indonesian military, trained and backed by the US, provoked a leftist coup against its leader, General Suharto. When the coup failed, the military used it as an excuse to depose Sukarno and replace him with Suharto. (According to diplomatic documents, the coup was a setup to justify the military takeover.)

What followed—as depicted in the film *The Year of Living Dangerously*—is almost beyond belief. In just a few weeks, between five hundred thousand and a million Indonesians were put to death, many in a grisly fashion. (But don't worry— the Suharto regime assures us they were all Communists.) It was later learned that the death squads had been working from hit lists provided by the US State Department (the usual cover for CIA agents).

The 1965 massacre was only the beginning for Indonesia's new military regime. In 1975, its army invaded the tiny nation of East Timor, a former Portuguese colony which has the bad luck to own significant oil reserves.

From 1975 to 1999, between a quarter and a third of East Timor's inhabitants were slaughtered by the Indonesian military, with arms largely supplied and paid for by the US. On a per-capita basis, this was the greatest genocide since the Holocaust. Combined with the 1965 killings and other atrocities, it put Suharto in the first rank of twentieth-century mass murderers.

Following protests and pressure from the military, Suharto was deposed in 1998 and died, unprosecuted, ten years later. East Timor was finally granted full independence in 2002.

Hit #14: "Greece Is a Flea"

In April 1967, an election campaign was about to begin in Greece. The candidate favored to win was George Papandreou, a staunch anti-Communist. He'd previously served as prime minister but had been removed from power in 1965 by the king, with the assistance of the CIA.

His son Andreas was a bit more left-wing, an admirer of subversives like Hubert Humphrey and Adlai Stevenson. He'd mused publicly about Greece steering a more neutral course in the Cold War, and he had some misgivings—correct ones, as it turned out—about the autocratic nature of certain elements in the Greek military.

Both father and son were a bit too independent for US policymakers and showed troubling signs that they were less than completely subservient to US interests.

Two days before the election campaign was to begin, a group of colonels overthrew the government and established military rule. The leader of the coup had been on the CIA payroll for the previous fifteen years.

For the next six years, martial law held sway in the birthplace of democracy. Widespread censorship, routine use of torture, brutal beatings and killings by the government became standard. Among the offenses deemed worthy of torture was the possession of leaflets critical of the government. While being tortured, victims were taunted that they were beyond all help, since the colonels were supported by the power of the United States.

34

The official justification for the coup—and the hideous repression that followed—was that they were necessary to save the nation from a communist takeover. The Papandreous weren't communists, of course, but they were something much more dangerous—committed, independent nationalists.

President Lyndon Johnson neatly summarized our attitude toward people like that. When the Greek ambassador objected to Johnson's plan for settling a dispute concerning Cyprus, LBJ said: "Fuck your parliament and your constitution. America is an elephant. Cyprus is a flea. Greece is a flea. If these two fleas continue itching the elephant, they may just get whacked by the elephant's trunk, whacked good. . . . If your prime minister gives me talk about democracy, parliament and constitutions, he, his parliament and his constitution may not last very long."

Hit #15:
The Martin Luther King Assassination

After being sentenced to 99 years for assassinating Martin Luther King, Jr, James Earl Ray said he'd been coerced into pleading guilty by his Mob-connected lawyer. He insisted he was framed for the King murder by a mysterious man named Raoul, for whom he'd been working in the spring of 1968, just before the assassination.

Certainly there's something fishy about the idea that Ray acted alone. He eluded a massive, three-and-a-half-month, international manhunt, escaping to Europe by way of Canada. This required *a lot* more cunning and financial resources than an incompetent, small-time thief and drifter like Ray could muster.

But the fishiest thing about Ray's escape was the four very detailed and precise aliases he used. All were the names of men who lived in the same section of Toronto (where Ray had never been) and each man bore a strong physical resemblance to Ray, right down to their scars. In at least one case, Ray also seems to have had access to information that could only have come from the alias' military records.

In 1989, a convicted murderer named Jules Kimble shed some light on all this. He claimed he'd been part of a conspiracy to kill King that included members of the CIA, the FBI and the Mafia.

Kimble says he introduced Ray to a CIA identities expert in Montreal in 1967, who provided Ray with the aliases he used as a fugitive. Investigators discovered that a CIA identities expert was indeed working in Montreal at that time. His name? Raoul Miora.

This alone ought be enough to reopen the case, but there's more to Kimble's story. He says that after meeting with Raoul, he took Ray to a CIA training camp, and later to Memphis, where a seven-man hit squad assassinated King.

Kimble claims Ray was part of the conspiracy, but was framed for the murder by means of a bundle of his belongings which was left at the scene of the crime. In the bundle was the supposed murder weapon with Ray's prints on it. (In other words, like Lee Harvey Oswald, he was "just the patsy.")

Kimble was connected with both Mob and intelligence figures during the period in question, including David Ferrie, a prime suspect in the JFK assassination (see Hit #9). The official account of Ray's supposed activities has more holes in it than a piece of cheesecloth. (See the *Sources* section for more details.)

Hit #16:

The Robert Kennedy Assassination

Hundreds of books have been written about whether there was a conspiracy in the JFK assassination. In the murder of his brother, Senator Robert Kennedy, the case for conspiracy can be summed up in one sentence: The Los Angeles coroner's report states that RFK was killed by a *point-blank shot from behind*, while everyone agrees that Sirhan Sirhan, the convicted assassin, was *at least three feet in front of him.*

There's a lot of evidence of CIA involvement in the RFK assassination. For one thing, despite the clear fact that there had to be a second gunman, the Los Angeles Police Department's special task force investigating the case bent over backwards to prove Sirhan was the lone assassin. Witnesses were intimidated, evidence was destroyed and plausible suspects weren't questioned.

Two key members of the task force had long-standing ties to the CIA and were especially zealous about browbeating witnesses whose testimony suggested a conspiracy. They got very upset when anyone mentioned the famous "girl in the polka-dot dress" (who was seen fleeing the scene of the crime shouting, "We shot him!") and they made sure that any mention of her was eliminated from the testimony.

Another obvious suspect who was barely investigated was the Rev. Jerry Owen, who was seen with Sirhan in the days before the murder. Owen admitted knowing Mafia courier Edgar Bradley, who also was present at the JFK assassination (see Hit #9). Bradley, who was actually arrested in Dealey Plaza, then released without being charged, appears to be linked to other key figures in the JFK case.

Then there's the late Dr. William Bryan, Jr, a hypnosis expert involved with the CIA's mind control experiments (see Hit #5). Bryan liked to brag of the famous subjects he had worked on—including, reportedly, Sirhan, who was extraordinarily susceptible to hypnosis. The name of another famous Bryan patient, the Boston Strangler, inexplicably turns up in Sirhan's notebooks.

Sirhan claims to have no memory of shooting at RFK or writing in his notebooks, and he appears to be telling the truth. Witnesses to the crime report that he seemed to be in some sort of trance.

More attention should also be focused on Thane Cesar, a security guard with right-wing, Mob and CIA connections who was standing directly behind RFK and who admitted he drew his gun.

Finally, one-time CIA man Robert Morrow wrote a book alleging that an agent of Iran's SAVAK (see Hit #3) was hired to kill RFK.

Hit #17: **Destroying Chilean Democracy**

In 1973, the CIA destroyed the oldest functioning democracy in South America, and it's still
trying to deny its involvement. The agency inter-
vened massively in Chile's 1958 and 1964 elections. In 1970, its fears were realized—the
socialist candidate, a physician named Salvador
Allende, was elected president.

Horrified, President Nixon ordered the CIA to
prevent Allende's inauguration. The agency did
its best to promote a military coup, but the
Chilean military's long history of respect for the
democratic process made this virtually impossible. One of the main impediments was the
Chilean army's chief of staff, General Rene
Schneider, so the CIA plotted with fanatics in
the military to assassinate him. The killing
backfired, solidifying support for Allende, who
took office as scheduled.

That approach having failed, the CIA was
ordered to create a "coup climate." ("Make the
economy scream," President Nixon told CIA
Director Helms.) CIA-backed acts of sabotage
and terror multiplied. The agency trained members of the fascist organization Patria y Libertad
(PyL) in guerrilla warfare and bombing, and they
were soon waging a campaign of arson.

The CIA also sponsored demonstrations and
strikes, funded by ITT and other US corpora-
tions with Chilean holdings. CIA-linked media,
including the country's largest newspaper,
fanned the flames of crisis. The military's patri-
otism was gradually eroded by endless stories
about Marxist "atrocities" like castration and
cannibalism, and rumors that the military
would be purged or "destroyed" and Soviet
bases set up.

When the coup finally came, in September 1973, it was led by the most extreme fascist members of the military, and it was unrelenting in its ferocity. Allende was taken out—whether by his own hand or another's, we may never know— though it's tough to kill yourself with a machine gun. Several cabinet ministers were also assassinated, the universities were put under military control, opposition parties were banned and thousands of Chileans were tortured and killed (many fingered as "radicals" on lists provided by the CIA).

Under the military junta headed by General Pinochet, torture of dissidents became routine, particularly at a gruesome prison called Colonia Dignidad. It drew expatriate Nazis from all over South America, one of whom told a victim that the good work started in the Nazi death camps was being continued there.

No wonder the CIA tries to deny it was involved in the Chilean coup. It turned a democratic, peace-loving nation into a slaughterhouse.

Hit #18: *Vietnam 1964–75*

Following the deaths of JFK (see Hit #9) and Ngo Dinh Diem (see Hit #10), it was only a matter of time before US combat troops became involved in Vietnam. Within days of the JFK assassination in November 1963, President Johnson had reversed JFK's plan to withdraw US personnel by the end of 1965. As LBJ told one impatient general, "Just get me elected; you can have your damn war."

In August 1964, the CIA and related military intelligence agencies helped fabricate a phony Vietnamese attack in the Gulf of Tonkin off North Vietnam. This supposed act of North Vietnamese aggression was used as the basis for escalating US involvement.

In March 1965, US troops began pouring into Vietnam. Nine years of backing the French, another nine years of backing Diem and two more years of CIA operations had failed. From this point on, the US Army took over the war effort.

Since the Vietnamese people overwhelmingly supported their own National Liberation Front (the NLF, which we called "Viet Cong"), the Army began destroying villages, herding people into internment camps, weeding out the leaders and turning the countryside into a "free-fire zone" (in other words, shoot anything that moves).

The CIA still had a role to play, however. Called Operation Phoenix, it was an assassination program, plain and simple. The idea was to cripple the NLF by killing influential people like mayors, teachers, doctors, tax collectors—anyone who aided the functioning of the NLF's parallel government in the South.

Many of the "suspects" were tortured, and some were tossed from helicopters during interrogation. William Colby, the CIA official in charge of Phoenix (he later became director of the CIA), insisted this was all part of "military necessity"—though he admitted to Congress that he really had no idea how many of the 20,000 killed were Viet Cong and how many were "loyal" Vietnamese.

Colby's confusion was understandable, since Phoenix was a joint operation between the US and the South Vietnamese, who used it as a means of extortion, a protection racket and a way to settle vendettas. Significantly, the South Vietnamese estimated the Operation Phoenix death toll at closer to 40,000. Whatever the exact number, there's no question the killings were necessary—after all, we were trying to prevent a bloodbath.

Hit #19: *The Secret War in Laos*

Between 1957 and 1965, Laotian governments came and went at a frantic pace, with the CIA sponsoring at least one coup a year. The problem was that a leftist group called the Pathet Lao kept getting enough votes to be included in coalition governments.

If the Pathet Lao or other leftists were voted into office, there'd either be a right-wing coup or the legislature would be dissolved, with future elections canceled if possible. If there was an election, the CIA would stuff ballot boxes, run propaganda campaigns and bribe legislators to try to get their candidates elected.

But the CIA didn't rely primarily on such namby-pamby techniques. Starting in the late 1950s, they recruited a mercenary force of some 40,000 men to attack Pathet Lao forces. Known as the Armée Clandestine ("secret army"), about half its members were from Thailand; the rest came from Taiwan, South Korea and other US client states. Despite the size of the Armée Clandestine, the Pathet Lao had enough support in the countryside to withstand it.

By 1964, after another CIA coup succeeded in installing a right-wing puppet, the Pathet Lao was completely frozen out of the electoral process. They'd begun receiving aid from the neighboring North Vietnamese, who were concerned about CIA-backed sabotage and assassination teams operating from Laotian territory. When the Pathet Lao made significant advances, the US military got directly—but secretly—involved.

From 1965 to 1973, the US dropped over *two million tons* of bombs on Laos, far more than all sides dropped in World War II. The bombing was so ferocious that over a quarter of the population became refugees, with many people living in caves for years at a time.

Since this CIA-run war in Laos was "secret," it only received a fraction of the attention given to the war in Vietnam. The secrecy proved unfortunate for many of the US soldiers involved.

If killed, they were listed as casualties of the Vietnam War. But when the Pathet Lao finally took power in 1975, no prisoner exchange treaty was signed, because we couldn't admit we'd been running a secret war in Laos.

Many of the Americans known to have been captured alive in Laos were involved in drug trafficking with the Armée Clandestine. If any are still alive, the CIA would have a considerable interest in denying their existence.

Hit #20: *Carpetbombing Cambodia*

In 1955, when CIA intervention in Cambodia began, there was no Communist threat to rationalize it. Sandwiched between two US client states (Thailand and South Vietnam), Prince Norodom Sihanouk, the popular sovereign of Cambodia, had one overriding goal—to keep his country from becoming involved in the Vietnam War. To that end, he stuck tenaciously to a policy of neutrality from 1955 to 1970, accepting aid from both Communist and capitalist states but criticizing each on occasion.

Sihanouk dismissed as fraudulent CIA documents that predicted imminent Communist aggression against him, but the plots and coup attempts by US-backed factions were all too real. In his memoir, *My War with the CIA*, Sihanouk alleges at least two assassination plots against him. There were also numerous incursions by Thai, South Vietnamese and US troops, a 1958 CIA-backed coup attempt and countless "accidental" bombing runs into Cambodian territory. Sihanouk's unwillingness to join the crusade against Communism made him the CIA's enemy.

Perhaps the final straw was when Sihanouk denounced US military incursions into Cambodia at a major press conference (dutifully, the US media barely mentioned his charges). In March 1970, Sihanouk was deposed by a CIA puppet named Lon Nol, who immediately began committing Cambodian troops to the war in Vietnam.

With Sihanouk out of the way, war quickly engulfed Cambodia. US bombing intensified near the Vietnamese border, driving North Vietnamese and NLF troops deeper into Cambodia (for more on the war in Vietnam, see Hit #18). From

1969 to 1975, US bombing killed 600,000 Cambodians and created a full-scale famine.

Not surprisingly, forces opposed to Lon Nol's regime grew rapidly. In 1975, one of them, the Communist Khmer Rouge, took power (before Lon Nol, they'd been a tiny, marginal group).

As depicted in the film *The Killing Fields,* the Khmer Rouge carried out many atrocities, probably executing 100,000 to 700,000 people. For propaganda purposes, Western reporters inflated the Khmer Rouge total by adding famine deaths to it, although they were actually the result of our bombing.

The Khmer Rouge's hideous crimes didn't prevent the CIA from supporting it after Vietnam invaded Cambodia in 1979, and for many years thereafter. As the Arabic saying goes, "The enemy of my enemy is my friend."

Hit #21: *Operation CHAOS*

In theory, the CIA's charter prohibits it from engaging in domestic operations. In practice, that requirement is totally ignored.

The CIA explains its massive presence on US campuses by saying that so many foreign students attend US universities, it would be a shame not to try to recruit them. The Domestic Contacts Division is needed to glean information from US tourists and business professionals returning from abroad. Then there's the Domestic Operations Division, which handles foreign interventions on US soil, like breaking into foreign embassies.

In order to do all that, the CIA has had to set up the same sort of network of phony businesses and front organizations it uses overseas. But the CIA claims that those are the only ways it operates domestically.

Unfortunately, even that's not true. From 1959 to at least 1974, the CIA used its domestic organizations to spy on thousands of US citizens whose only crime was disagreeing with their government's policies.

This picked up speed when FBI Director J. Edgar Hoover told President Johnson that nobody would be protesting his Vietnam War policies unless they were being directed to do so by some foreign power. Johnson ordered the CIA to investigate.

In response, the CIA vastly expanded its campus surveillance program and stepped up its liaisons with local police departments. It trained special intelligence units in major cities to carry out "black bag" jobs (break-ins, wiretaps, etc.) against US "radicals."

In 1968, the CIA's various domestic programs were consolidated and expanded under the code name Operation CHAOS. When Richard Nixon became president the following year, his administration enacted the Huston Plan, which called for even greater operations against "subversives," including wiretapping, break-ins, mail-opening, no-knock searches and "selective assassinations." Bureaucratic infighting tabled the plan, but much of it was implemented in other forms, not only by the CIA but also by the FBI and the Secret Service.

With the revelation of CIA and White House complicity in the Watergate break-in (see Hit #23), light began to shine on Operation CHAOS. After a period of "reform," much of CHAOS's work was privatized, and right-wing groups and "former" CIA agents now provide the bulk of the CIA's domestic intelligence.

Hit #22:

The World's Largest Drug Dealer

Even before the CIA was officially founded, it was intertwined with major drug-trafficking organizations—the organization it grew out of, the OSS, cooperated with the Mafia during World War II. After the war, one of the first covert operations of the new CIA was to break the strength of left-wing labor unions in southern France. To do this, the CIA cemented an ongoing tie with the Corsican Mafia, the biggest heroin traffickers in the world at that time.

By the early 1960s, much of the world's heroin production had shifted to Southeast Asia, thanks to another major CIA operation. The agency had trained Nationalist Chinese (i.e. Taiwanese) forces to invade mainland China; when that operation failed, they settled in northeastern Burma and became the world's largest opium producers—mainly by terrorizing the local villagers into growing it for them. Under Burma's government of military thugs, opium production continues today (although Afghanistan is now the world's largest source).

Meanwhile, as the US moved into Indochina (see Hits #18, 19 and 20), the existing opium trade there gradually became integrated into other US operations. While President Nixon, full of law-and-order rhetoric, was making a great show of busting the famous "French connection," his buddies in the Florida Mafia were moving into Vietnam. By 1970, the US was flooded with pure Asian heroin, some of it smuggled home inside the corpses of US soldiers!

In Laos, the CIA was running a 40,000-man mercenary army (see Hit #19). It included many Hmong tribespeople, who were longtime opium farmers. The CIA airline, Air America, ran weapons to the army and brought the Hmong's crop back out to market. Some of the massive profits from the operations were laundered by CIA agent Mike Hand through an Australian bank he founded (see Hit #38) and were used to finance other CIA operations behind Congress' back.

Many veterans of CIA drug operations in Asia went on to star in the agency's secret wars in Central America in the 1980s (see Hits #32, #33, #34 and #39), where the above pattern was repeated. The Nicaraguan Contras were partially funded by cocaine smuggled into the US on customs-free supply flights. CIA assets in Honduras, Costa Rica, El Salvador and Panama helped facilitate the trade.

In the CIA's wars in Afghanistan (see Hits #36 and #45), the Afghan rebels and their Pakistani hosts also partly financed themselves with profits from heroin. Much of their product ended up— once again—in the veins of US addicts.

Hit #23: *The Watergate Break-In*

In June 1972, a team of freelance spooks called the "plumbers" (because they were hired to fix leaks) broke into the headquarters of the Democratic National Committee at the Watergate office complex in Washington. No one knows exactly what they were looking for. Some theories center on Nixon's need to find out what kind of blackmail the Democrats had on him; others say it was a case of Nixon and the CIA trying to blackmail each other; and there are several other intriguing CIA connections.

The Watergate break-in was so badly mishandled that some people think it was deliberately botched. The man doing the botching was James McCord, onetime chief of security for the CIA. He twice placed masking tape on a doorjamb in a way the Watergate guard couldn't miss. And it was McCord who wrote a letter to a federal judge, just as the affair was about to be swept under the rug, warning that "higher-ups" were covering up their involvement in Watergate.

One of the plumbers who went to jail, Howard Hunt—a longtime CIA officer and a player in the JFK assassination (see Hit #9)—successfully blackmailed Nixon for over one million dollars, but he may have pushed his luck too far. His wife, carrying a suitcase full of cash, was killed in a mysterious plane crash. Convincing evidence suggests the flight had been deliberately sabotaged.

Later, another CIA man, Alexander Butterfield, let slip to the Senate Watergate Committee that the president was in the habit of taping his Oval Office conversations, providing the final nail for Nixon's coffin. Butterfield, on leave from the CIA, had requested assignment to the White House.

Washington Post reporter Bob Woodward received dirt on Watergate from a secret source he called Deep Throat, a man clearly familiar with the intelligence community. (In 2005, high-ranking FBI official Mark Felt revealed that he was Deep Throat.) Woodward himself had been a top-security briefer for the Office of Naval Intelligence and both his editor Ben Bradlee and *Post* publisher Katherine Graham's late husband had also worked for the CIA.

Nixon told Chief of Staff Bob Haldeman to call off the CIA's Watergate investigation because it could "blow the whole Bay of Pigs thing." When Haldeman took this message to CIA Director Richard Helms, Helms erupted: "The Bay of Pigs had nothing to do with this!"

What were they talking about? According to Haldeman, "the Bay of Pigs" was Nixon's coded way of referring to the JFK assassination.

Hit #24: *The Mighty Wurlitzer*

Deputy Director Frank Wisner proudly referred to the CIA's worldwide propaganda machine as "the Mighty Wurlitzer" (for his ability to make the media play whatever tune he wanted). And indeed, the agency's skill at murdering people is matched only by its ability to murder the truth.

The CIA has published literally hundreds of books that spread its party line on the Cold War. It was particularly proud of *The Penkovsky Papers*, supposedly the memoirs of a KGB defector but actually completely ghostwritten by CIA scribes. A bit more embarrassing is Claire Sterling's *The Octopus*, which advanced the now-discredited theory that the Russians were behind the 1981 attempt on the life of Pope John Paul II. Even the popular *Fodor's Travel Guides* started as a CIA front.

The CIA also owns dozens of newspapers and magazines the world over. These not only provide cover for their agents but allow them to plant misinformation that regularly makes it back to the US through the wire services. (The CIA has even placed agents on guard at the wire services, to prevent inconvenient facts from being disseminated.)

In 1977, famed Watergate journalist Carl Bernstein revealed that over 400 US journalists had been employed by the CIA. These ranged from freelancers who were paid for regular debriefings to actual CIA officers who worked under deep cover. Nearly every major US news organization has had spooks on its payroll, usually with the cooperation of top management.

The three most valuable media assets the CIA could count on were William Paley's CBS, Arthur Sulzberger's *New York Times* and Henry Luce's *Time/Life* empire. All three bent over backwards to promote the picture of Oswald as a lone nut in the JFK assassination (see Hit #9).

Among prominent journalists who've worked knowingly with the CIA are the late *National Review* founder and talk-show host William F. Buckley, PBS interviewer Bill Moyers, the late columnist Stewart Alsop, former *Washington Post* editor Ben Bradlee and *Ms.* magazine founder Gloria Steinem.

Bernstein's landmark article on the CIA and the media told of the agency's frantic efforts to limit Congressional inquiry into the matter, with claims that "some of the biggest names in journalism could get smeared." And while the CIA director at the time, George H. W. Bush, made a not-too-convincing show of discontinuing the agency's manipulation of the media, it's clear that the CIA still regards the space between your ears as one of its most important battlefields.

Hit #25: **Mass Murder in Angola**

In terms of the ratio of blood spilled to goals achieved (if those goals can even be determined), the intervention in Angola is a strong candidate for the most pointless CIA operation ever.

In 1975, the collapse of the Portuguese empire left its African colony of Angola with three groups struggling for power. Each had at various times flirted with both capitalism and Marxism, and each had taken aid from both the East and the West. Congo (a US ally, then called Zaire) backed one faction, the Soviets backed another (the MPLA) and the CIA ended up backing the third, Jonas Savimbi's UNITA.

The main reason for the CIA's involvement in Angola was Henry Kissinger's determination to start another war as soon as possible after the fall of Saigon, to show the world how tough we were. We said we were worried about oil—even though there isn't much of it in Angola, and the MPLA, which controlled the oil from 1975 on, continued to sell it to the West throughout the war. Another absurd excuse was also given: Angola is close to "shipping lanes" (as is every coastal nation on earth).

No diplomatic option was ever pursued by Kissinger; instead, the CIA put untold amounts of blood and treasure behind Savimbi, a brutal, bloodthirsty autocrat. Our determination to turn Angola into a Cold War battlefield brought in South African troops, who supported Savimbi, and—in response—Cuban troops, who supported the MPLA (with great success).

South Africa's involvement was part of its efforts to destabilize all of its neighbors, in order to delay the inevitable ascension of its black majority to power. Since it was our faction they were supporting, this caused considerable damage to US relations with black Africa.

FINE ANGOLAN HORSES — TAKE YOUR PICK

After $40 million and thousands of corpses, Congress—in a rare display of principle—cut off funds for the Angolan War in 1976, the first time it had ever voted to shut down a CIA operation. Unfortunately, the CIA managed to sustain the killing off the books until Reagan took office in 1981. Then millions more dollars and thousands more lives were wasted until, in 1990, the ongoing Angolan stalemate at last resulted in an election.

When Savimbi lost overwhelmingly to the MPLA, he cranked the war right back up again, initially with further CIA funding. Finally, in 1993, the US distanced itself from him and recognized the MPLA, but the war still continued. By the time a cease-fire was finally reached in 2002, more than 500,000 Angolans had been killed and another four million were internal refugees.

Hit #26:
The Orlando Letelier Assassination

"Are you the wife of Orlando Letelier?" asked the anonymous caller. "Yes," she answered. "No," the caller said, "you are his widow."

A week later, on September 21, 1976, the exiled Chilean diplomat and prominent critic of the CIA-backed Pinochet regime (see Hit #17) was torn to pieces by a car bomb on the streets of Washington. Also killed was Letelier's American aide, Ronni Moffitt. Her husband, Michael, was blown clear of the car; he immediately began shouting that Chilean fascists were responsible for the atrocity.

He was right, but those fascists had powerful allies in Washington. An FBI informant knew of the plot to assassinate Letelier before the fact but the FBI did nothing to protect him. After the bombing, CIA Director George H. W. Bush told

the FBI that there'd been no Chilean involvement whatever. The CIA was certain of this, he
said, because it had many reliable sources
inside the Chilean secret police, DINA.

Actually, the CIA had known that a DINA hit
squad was in the US and headed for
Washington. After the bombing, the agency
purged its files of photos of the assassins. The
CIA and DINA then began planting stories in the
press suggesting that Letelier had been killed by
leftists seeking to make a martyr of him.

The FBI figured out the identities of Letelier's
assassins within weeks, but didn't charge them
until the CIA's cover-up unraveled several years
later. The unraveling began a month after the
killing, when a Cuban airliner was bombed,
killing 73 passengers. That bombing was done
by a violent group of CIA-linked Cuban exiles
who were connected with the Bay of Pigs and
the JFK assassination (see Hits #8 and #9) and
who went on to do similar things in El Salvador
and Nicaragua (see Hits #32 and #33).

In 2000, the CIA admitted that the mastermind
of the Letelier/Moffitt asssassination, Chilean
Intelligence Chief Manuel Contreras, was a paid
CIA asset, and that it had consulted him about
the attack in October 1976.

Apologists argue that no one can prove that
Letelier's convicted assassins, "former" CIA
agent Michael Townley and two Cuban exiles,
were acting under agency orders. But if they
weren't, why did the CIA immediately begin covering up for them?

This case is so complex that, in 1991, the
(post-Pinochet) Chilean Supreme Court asked
then-President George H. W. Bush if he'd mind
submitting to questioning. You'd better believe
he minded.

Hit #27: *Exaggerating the Soviet Threat*

In 1949, influential Republican senator Arthur Vandenberg of Michigan told President Truman that if he wanted to justify massive Cold War military spending, he'd have to "scare the hell out of the American people." That's a mission the CIA has always taken to heart. From the very beginning, it's overestimated Soviet military strength, in part because of its dependence on the Gehlen Org for intelligence about Eastern Europe (see Hit #1).

There were many subtle ways of cooking the books. One was to estimate Soviet spending as though their soldiers were paid as much as US personnel, though in fact they received far less. Another was to release misleading data on how much larger Soviet missiles were than ours (which actually meant they were more primitive) or to compare missile capabilities based on the Soviets' greater "throw weight" (which was needed to push their huge, inaccurate missiles). Some reports pretended that the entire Soviet military was poised to invade Europe, when much of it was actually defending their Chinese border.

There was, in fact, a group of CIA analysts who had a fairly sophisticated understanding of the actual capabilities of—and factions within—the USSR, but they were regarded as dangerous pinkos by the hawks within the agency. Some of these hawks served on the Committee on the Present Danger (CPD), a private group that lobbied for massive hikes in military spending and that backed Ronald Reagan for president in 1976.

When George H. W. Bush (who'd been a CIA asset since the late 1950s) became CIA director in 1975, one of his duties was to oversee a project called Team B. This was an offering from

President Ford to the CPD and other right-wingers who argued that CIA analysts were underestimating Soviet military strength and who wanted a second opinion.

The CIA analysts regarded Bush's backing of Team B to rewrite their data as a betrayal, but Reagan rewarded Bush by making him his running mate in 1980. Once elected, Reagan named every one of the Team B members to sensitive military posts and jacked up the Pentagon budget.

When Bush became president in 1989, he chose as his CIA director Robert Gates, who'd been the leader of the pro-Team B faction in the CIA during Bush's tenure as director. Gates had spent the Reagan years providing seriously distorted intelligence estimates of Soviet strength, which may be why the CIA was so woefully unprepared to anticipate the collapse of the USSR in 1991.

Hit #28: **Mass Murder at Jonestown**

There's lots of evidence that the mass murder at Jonestown, Guyana, in 1978 was the culmination of a massive and barbarous CIA behavior control experiment. And mass murder is what it was—not mass suicide, as widely reported. The Guyanese coroner's report states that the 913 victims didn't drink the mythical cyanide-laced Kool-Aid—there was no trace of cyanide in their bodies. Eighty to ninety percent of the victims had been injected with other lethal agents, while the rest were shot. The coroner concluded that only two had committed suicide.

Cult leader Jim Jones had long-standing ties to the CIA, stretching back to his boyhood friendship with the notorious CIA torture expert Dan Mitrione. Mitrione regarded torture as an art form and, while instructing security forces in Brazil and Uruguay, he had beggars kidnapped so he could practice on them. Mitrione's old pal Jones was in Brazil at the same time, and he made frequent trips to the CIA headquarters in Belo Horizonte.

Jones returned from Brazil to found the People's Temple in Ukiah, California. Early on he engaged in shocking abuses of his cult members. He also used them to infiltrate the organizations of liberal politicians, where they raillied voters and thus made the politicians beholden to him. San Francisco Mayor George Moscone and Supervisor Harvey Milk, both assassinated a week after Jonestown, owed political favors to Jones. So did the district attorney whose lenient prosecution of the assassin allowed him to get off with only a token sentence.

When reports began to surface of murders tied to the People's Temple, Jones fled with his flock to Guyana, whose prime minister owed his job to a 1964 CIA coup. Jones was in close touch with CIA agents at the US Embassy in Guyana, at least one of whom was at Jonestown at the time of the massacre.

Survivors report that Jonestown was a virtual concentration camp where the mostly black cultists worked like slaves. They were beaten, tortured, raped and given massive doses of both verbal indoctrination and drugs. Many of the mind-altering substances used in the MK-ULTRA program (see Hit #5) were found at Jonestown, in amounts sufficient to subdue a city of 200,000.

The end came when Rep. Leo Ryan, a key congressional opponent of the CIA, arrived to investigate and was assassinated by Jones' followers. Then the mass killings began (though Jones' wealthy white lieutenants escaped unharmed). Millions in cash were found at the site, but the bulk of Jones' fortune, estimated at $2 billion, disappeared into secret bank accounts. As for Jones himself, photographs of what are supposed to be his body don't show his tattoos.

Hit #29: **The October Surprise**

When Ronald Reagan was running for president against Jimmy Carter in 1980, 52 American hostages were being held in Iran. The Reagan/Bush campaign feared that if the hostages were released before the November election, the resulting "October Surprise" might help Carter win.

According to former Iranian President Banisadr, Reagan officials met with the Iranians in Paris in October 1980 and gave them $40 million in exchange for agreeing to hold the hostages until after the election. (Some sources also say former CIA Director George H. W. Bush and/or future CIA Director William Casey attended those meetings.)

October Surprise was also the name of a network of current and former CIA agents within Reagan's campaign whose job was to obtain intelligence from the Carter White House. It was a sophisticated—and ultimately successful—effort to destabilize the Carter administration.

The October Surprise team stole briefing books and other documents from the White House. They also leaked a series of fabricated stories to the media regarding Carter's negotiations with Iran and/or plans for a hostage rescue, which made both tasks considerably more difficult.

When Carter eventually did mount a hostage rescue, someone gave the Iranians—and William Casey—details about the operation in advance. It ended in disaster, with no one rescued and eight American soldiers dead.

Despite the October Surprise team's high-powered disinformation campaign, Carter managed to make a deal with the Iranians that didn't include trading arms for hostages (see Hit #34).

But after the meeting with Reagan officials in Paris, the Iranians backed out. The hostages weren't released until the very day of Reagan's inauguration—and millions of dollars in weaponry began flowing to Iran shortly thereafter.

The October Surprise deal has been subject to more disinformation and manipulation than any operation since the JFK assassination (see Hit #9). Several key witnesses have met untimely deaths, as did one reporter who found links to other Reagan-era covert operations.

Finally, a Warren-Commission-like congressional investigation concluded that there was "no evidence" of a conspiracy. Unfortunately, there are several glaring errors in the report, and there's plenty of evidence that was never looked at. Notably, a Russian government report that was hidden from the committee surfaced in 2010, corroborating many of the charges.

Hit #30:
Libya and Our Bogeyman Gaddafi

In April 1980, CIA agents Edwin Wilson and Frank Terpil were indicted for providing weapons and training to the regime of Libyan strongman Muammar Gaddafi. The CIA says that Terpil and Wilson were "rogue elephants" but Wilson, who is currently serving a life sentence in a federal penitentiary, claims he was acting under orders.

Wilson's claim is worth taking seriously. Many other members of the operation received slaps on the wrist and continued to work for the US government; some went on to be players in the Iran/Contra scandal (see Hit #34). The plastic explosives provided to Gaddafi may have been used in a number of CIA-connected bombings, including the assassination of Orlando Letelier (see Hit #26).

Gaddafi long enjoyed the status of official US bogeyman. He stayed firmly entrenched in this role while others, like Noriega and Saddam, waxed and waned. Yet Gaddafi also received weapons and training from the British and the Germans, and was said to own 15% of the stock of Fiat, the largest company in Italy and a major Western defense contractor.

The circumstances of Gaddafi's rise to power in a 1969 coup are also curious. Despite the vast amounts of oil wealth involved, Nixon and Kissinger lifted nary an eyebrow when Gaddafi ousted the pro-Western Libyan monarch. Immediately thereafter, Gaddafi began agitating for higher oil prices.

The Nixon administration announced that Gaddafi's suggested price hike was "justified" and the Shah of Iran (see Hit #3) agreed. The resulting surge in oil prices not only enriched the multinational oil companies but allowed the Shah to purchase billions in US arms, which he used to fulfill his role as regional policeman for the US.

If Gaddafi was actually a Western agent provocateur, it would hardly have been unprecedented. Several radical Arab terrorists appear to be working both sides of the street (see Hit #35), while many other Arab heads of state have been on the CIA payroll.

But even if Gaddafi was just what he seemed to be—a thoroughly demented Arab nationalist—that still doesn't necessarily negate Wilson's claim. The CIA may have been infiltrating Gaddafi's regime in order to manipulate him for their own ends, and the operation may simply have blown up in their face (as have so many others).

After switching sides several more times, Gaddafi was finally deposed and killed by a NATO-backed rebellion in 2011.

Hit #31: *Invading Grenada*

Here's what the US public was told: President Reagan woke up one day to discover that a horrible Marxist coup had taken over the Caribbean island of Grenada. Because there were Cuban troops on the island, the president had to send the US military to rescue US citizens trapped there and held as virtual hostages.

There was no way to get a more accurate picture, since the US military kept reporters from setting foot on Grenada during the invasion; a boatload of US journalists was turned away at gunpoint and all flights in and out were canceled. Much later, long after everyone had stopped paying attention to Grenada, it became clear that the official story was built on a mountain of lies.

The CIA began destabilizing Grenada in 1979, when a man named Maurice Bishop (no relation to the spook mentioned in Hit #9) ousted the eccentric thug who ruled the island. Bishop set to work developing a better life for Grenada's citizens and earned much popular support for doing so. But he ran afoul of the US fairly quickly, when he failed to join in the quarantine of Cuba.

The final straw was Bishop's mildly socialist program (private enterprise left unmolested, but free healthcare, school lunches, etc.). Before long, a CIA propaganda campaign was portraying Grenada as a terrorist state allied to the Soviet Union, its 100,000 inhabitants armed to the teeth and poised to attack the pitifully vulnerable US.

The US invasion was planned at least two years before it happened, and CIA acts of sabotage proliferated. Money was given to opposition politicians and neighboring armies. Finally,

in late 1983, extremists in his own party over-
threw Bishop and executed him, and the US
invasion began. CIA agents among the
"hostages" helped coordinate the three-day war
over shortwave radio.

As for the Cuban troops we invaded to protect
our citizens from, there were 43 of them; the
other Cubans on Grenada were mostly middle-
aged construction workers. The Cubans let it be
known that they would not interfere with the US
"rescue," but the US troops fired on them and
they defended themselves. That night, the US
assured Cuba that its citizens in Grenada were
"not a target"; the next day, we attacked them
with helicopter gunships. When it was all over,
81 Cubans, 296 Grenadines and 131 Americans
had been killed or wounded.

Today Grenada is back where it was before
Bishop, mired in poverty and hopelessness. But,
hey, it's no longer a threat to our very survival.

Hit #32: *Destroying El Salvador*

The fourteen families who ruled El Salvador had never been squeamish about taking the lives of anyone who got in their way. Among the many people who commonly got in their way are the Catholic clergy, due to the concern they often showed for the poor. As a result, a popular slogan among right-wing Salvadorans was: "Be patriotic—kill a priest."

In 1980, El Salvador's archbishop, Oscar Romero, made the mistake of taking President Carter's human rights rhetoric seriously. He wrote Carter, begging him to stop military support for El Salvador's murderous rulers. Carter ignored Romero, but the people who ran El Salvador didn't. Shortly after he sent the letter, Romero was shot through the heart while saying Mass.

Romero's assassination was ordered by Roberto D'Aubuisson (daw-bwee-SAWN), nicknamed "Blowtorch Bob" for his favorite torture tool. A big admirer of Adolf Hitler, D'Aubuisson once said,

"You Germans were very intelligent. You realized that the Jews were responsible for the spread of Communism and you began to kill them."

All in all, about 75,000 Salvadorans were killed between 1979 and the signing of peace accords in 1992. D'Aubuisson died in 1992 but his ARENA party, supported by the US, stayed in power until 2009. Its many human-rights abuses remain unpunished.

D'Aubuisson was a big wheel in the World Anti-Communist League (now called the World League for Freedom and Democracy). Organized in 1961, it serves as an international umbrella organization for extreme-right militants. Among its members are expatriate Nazis, Italian terrorists, Japanese fascists, racist Afrikaners, Latin American death squad leaders and a number of US congressmen and "former" CIA agents.

Aside from participating in this evil organization, the CIA did much else to encourage bloodshed in El Salvador. With billions of dollars of US military aid at its disposal, it flew air raids, waded into combat and trained the military units that formed the death squads.

The agency's spin doctors also worked to improve the government's image. This often consisted of denying that atrocities like the 1982 massacre at El Mozote ever happened. Agency sycophants in the media parroted this line shamelessly until, in 1993, a UN Truth Commission investigated El Mozote and determined that 733 peasants had been murdered there.

In 1982, after he was no longer president, Jimmy Carter called El Salvador's government the "bloodthirstiest in the hemisphere." It's too bad he didn't come to that realization back when he—like his predecessors and successors—was funding it.

Hit #33: **Destroying Nicaragua**

FDR once said about Nicaragua's dictator: "Somoza may be a son of a bitch, but he's *our* son of a bitch." So when a later Somoza (the son of "our son of a bitch") was overthrown in 1979, we spared no effort until Nicaragua was ours again.

When President Carter saw that the younger Somoza's days were numbered, he tried to ease him out of power, unaware that retired CIA agents were providing him with further weaponry. Carter's plan was to keep Somoza's private army, the National Guard, in power, while Somoza escaped to enjoy his $900–million fortune (until he was assassinated in Argentina).

Most Nicaraguans, having suffered 46 years of the Guard's unrelenting brutality, were not thrilled with that plan. When Somoza fell, so did his hated National Guard.

Many of the Guard were evacuated on US planes. We reassembled them, armed and supplied them, had them trained by Argentinian death squads and sent them back to harass the new regime. Because the Guard was so despised in Nicaragua, they were given a new name—the *Contras* (an abbreviation of the Spanish word for *counter-revolutionaries*).

The resulting bloodshed was perhaps the least covert of all CIA covert operations. President Reagan was perfectly candid about the goals—the second-poorest nation in the hemisphere should be "pressured" until "they say 'uncle.'"

The methods became part of the public record too—though not intentionally—when the CIA's *Freedom Fighters Manual* was leaked to the press. It gave detailed instructions on assassination, sabotage, kidnapping, blackmail and the slaughter of civilians.

The US lavished military and financial aid on the Contras, whom they used to terrorize rural Nicaragua. Since many peasants were delighted that the new government was providing them with teachers and doctors (for the first time ever), the Contras targeted doctors and teachers in particular.

The CIA mined harbors and blew up fuel tanks, then told the Contras to claim credit. The agency flew supplies to the Contras, attempted to assassinate the Nicaraguan leadership and pumped millions of dollars into opposition politicians. And, as in Chile, they made the economy "scream" (see Hit #17).

Finally, in 1989, after ten years of warfare—both economic and military—the Nicaraguans gave up and voted for the US-backed slate of candidates. If any of them wondered what would happen should they fail to do so, they only needed to look south to Panama, which had just been invaded by the US the month before (see Hit #39).

Hit #34: *The Iran/Contra Operation*

The Reagan administration brought out the worst in the CIA—its tendency to distort intelligence to justify policies, its fanatical enthusiasm for covert action, and its disdain for congressional oversight. Reagan's CIA director, William Casey, was running so many off-the-books operations that he gutted the agency's own counterintelligence division out of fear that it would find out what he was up to. This made it absurdly easy for moles and traitors to continue operating, and led to an embarrassing series of spy scandals that continue to this day.

The most famous of these was Iran/Contra, which began with a series of arms deals with the Muslim theocracy of Iran. The weapons shipments began in March 1981, years before there were any new hostages to trade arms for. This lends credence to the theory that the arms were actually a payoff for the October Surprise deal (see Hit #29).

Oliver North and his cronies charged the Iranians ridiculously high markups on the weapons they sold them, and some profits from this were used to buy arms for the Nicaraguan Contras (see Hit #33), in blatant defiance of a Congressional ban. (Actually, more of the money ended up in private bank accounts than ever reached the Contras.)

All CIA covert actions are supposed to be authorized by a presidential "finding," but Iran/Contra ran for years without one. Once the participants realized they were committing impeachable offenses, they had the president sign a "retroactive finding." It was later destroyed, to protect Reagan.

Because the half-hearted Congressional probe into Iran/Contra had secretly agreed in advance to avoid any evidence that might lead to Reagan's impeachment, it hardly scratched the surface. For example, it barely touched on the CIA's involvement in Contra drug trafficking (see Hit #22), nor did it delve into covert manipulation of US elections using a variety of secret funds—even though several US representatives opposed to the Contra war were defeated as a result of it.

The Iran/Contra operation set up something called the Office of Public Diplomacy, which used taxpayers' own money to convince them that the CIA's secret wars were a great idea. (This was really just an aboveground example of the CIA's normal propaganda efforts, as described in Hit #24.)

Probably the most dangerous part of the whole Iran/Contra mess was Oliver North's draft of a plan to suspend the US Constitution in case of anti-war protests. One congressman tried to ask about this, but was gaveled down and told it could be only discussed in "executive session."

Hit #35: *The Crash of Pan Am 103*

Syrian terrorist Monzer al-Kassar had a great setup: An accomplice at the Frankfurt airport regularly substituted a suitcase full of heroin for an identical suitcase checked onto a Pan Am flight to New York. This operation netted al-Kassar millions and—as payback for his serving as a middleman in Oliver North's Iran/Contra deals (see Hit #34)—the CIA protected it.

The CIA also hoped that al-Kassar would use his influence to secure the release of US hostages in Beirut. But Major Charles McKee, the CIA agent charged with rescuing the hostages, was outraged when he heard of this arrangement, which he felt could jeopardize his mission. He complained bitterly, but got no reply. Impulsively, and against procedures, McKee and four other members of his team decided to fly home—on Pan Am Flight 103—to expose the al-Kassar deal at CIA headquarters.

On December 20, 1989, a German government agent in Frankfurt who was privy to the heroin deal noticed that the switched suitcase being put onto Flight 103 looked completely different than it usually did. Aware that a bomb threat had been made against the flight, he called his local CIA contact and asked what was up. "Don't worry about it," he was told. "Don't stop it. Let it go."

When Pan Am 103 blew up over Lockerbie, Scotland, killing 270 people, a CIA team was on its way to the crash site within the hour. Disguised as Pan Am employees, they removed evidence, then later returned it—or materials that looked like it—to be rediscovered.

Initial suspicions focused on Syria and Iran, with the possible motive being revenge for an

Iranian passenger plane that had been shot down by a US warship the previous July. But when Syria's cooperation was needed during the First Iraq War (see Hit #40), the blame was shifted to our favorite whipping boy, Libya (see Hit #30).

Two Libyans were tried and one was convicted in 2001, though there's plenty of evidence that the trial was a sham. The convicted man was released in 2009 on "humanitarian grounds," to considerable uproar. During the Libyan revolution of 2011, a defecting official claimed that strongman Muammar Gaddafi had been behind the bombing, but no further evidence was offered.

Pan Am's own investigation had uncovered the links to al-Kassar, but the CIA refused to release relevant documents, and Pan Am lost a massive lawsuit filed by the families of Flight 103 victims. Soon after, it filed for bankruptcy.

Hit #36: **The First Afghan War**

During the Reagan years, the CIA ran nearly two dozen covert operations against various governments. Of these, Afghanistan was by far the biggest; it was, in fact, the biggest CIA operation up to that time, both in terms of dollars spent ($5–$6 billion) and personnel involved. Yet it not only generated little controversy, but enjoyed strong bipartisan support. That's because its main purpose was to "bleed" the Soviet Union, just as we had been bled in Vietnam.

Prior to the 1979 Russian invasion, Afghanistan was ruled by a brutal dictator. Like the neighboring Shah of Iran, he allowed the CIA to set up radar installations in his country that were used to monitor the Soviets. In 1979, after several dozen Soviet advisors were massacred by Afghan tribesmen, the USSR sent in the Red Army.

The Soviets tried to install a pliable client regime, without taking local attitudes much into account. Many of the mullahs who controlled chunks of Afghan territory objected to Soviet efforts to educate women and to institute land reform. Others, outraged by the USSR's attempts to suppress the heroin trade, shifted their operations to Pakistan (see Hit #22).

As for the CIA, its aim was simply to humiliate the Soviets by arming anyone who would fight against them. The agency funnelled cash and weapons to over a dozen guerrilla groups, many of whom had been staging raids from Pakistan years before the Soviet invasion. Today, long after the Soviet Union left Afghanistan (and, in fact, has ceased to exist), most of these groups are still fighting each other for control of the country.

Besides tossing billions of dollars into the conflict, the CIA transferred sensitive weapons technology to fanatical Muslim extremists, with consequences that will haunt the US for years to come. Two notable veterans of the Afghan war were Sheik Abdel-Rahman, famous for his role in the first World Trade Center bombing (in 1993), and Osama bin Laden.

The CIA succeeded in creating chaos but never developed a plan for *ending* it. When the ten-year war was over, a million people were dead, and Afghan heroin had captured 60% of the US market.

Hit #37: *The American Lake*

In 1993, US citizens were shocked to learn that their government had performed nuclear experiments on innocent and unknowing test subjects. To the residents of US-administered "trust territories" in the South Pacific, this was an old story.

Ever since we nuked Japan in August 1945, the US had regarded the Pacific as an "American lake." For years, both the US and France had hustled the natives out of the way, then tested nuclear weapons on, and lobbed missiles at, various Pacific islands under their "trusteeship."

Sometimes natives were returned prematurely to their irradiated homelands, resulting in birth defects and cancers. Not surprisingly, this led to particularly strong anti-nuclear sentiments among the Pacific islanders. Also not surprisingly, the CIA has done everything in its power to counter them.

The US occupied the tiny island of Palau (a.k.a. Belau) after World War II and, despite native calls for self-determination, we won't be departing anytime soon.

In 1979, the Palauans had the effrontery to pass the world's first anti-nuclear constitution. The response to that was countless beatings and assassinations of Palauan anti-nuclear activists, and *ten* subsequent elections, all sponsored by the US.

In 1994, we finally managed to get the Palauans to approve a "Compact of Free Association" that allows the US to park nuclear vessels in their ports—and to keep a military base on the island—until 2044.

The island nation of Kanaky (a.k.a. New Caledonia) has been occupied by French troops, since a bogus 1987 election that "ratified" French rule. Because Kanaky's exiled resistance movement received support from the island nation of Vanuatu (formerly called New Hebrides), which had one of the most progressive governments in the Pacific, the CIA funnelled money into destabilizing Vanuatu.

In 1991, they succeeded, and Vanuatu reversed its support of Kanaky independence. The UN officially calls Kanaky a "non-self-governing territory" but promises that it will be allowed to vote on changing that status sometime between 2014 and 2019.

In a 1987 election in Fiji, a progressive coalition replaced a pro-US government; less than a month later, a CIA-backed coup deposed the progressive coalition. CIA "coup experts"—including the head of the World Anti-Communist League (see Hit #32)—were on hand before, during and after the coup.

The new ruling junta purchased US helicopters to use against any Fijians who had the gall to imagine they have the right to elect whomever they please. In the quarter-century since then, Fiji has endured military governments that control the lucrative multinational trade in hardwoods.

Hit #38: **Setting Up Crooked Banks**

After British bank examiners first shut down its London branch in 1991, BCCI (the Bank of Credit and Commerce International) became known as "the world's crookedest bank"—or, as then-CIA Director Robert Gates called it, "the Bank of Crooks and Criminals International." He, of all people, would have known.

Throughout its entire history, the CIA has set up an elaborate shell game of "proprietaries" (front companies), money-laundering operations and off-the-books projects so complex that no outsider—and few insiders—could keep track of them. BCCI was neither the first nor the last of these.

An important predecessor was the Nugan Hand Bank (see Hit #22), which helped the CIA topple a pesky government in its host country, Australia. Founded by reputed Mafia associate Frank Nugan and former Green Beret Mike Hand, capitalized by drug and weapons deals in the last years of the Vietnam War, it helped finance agency operations in Angola and the Middle East.

Nugan Hand's board was loaded with spooks, including former CIA Director William Colby. When Australian bank examiners closed in on the bank in 1977, Nugan killed himself and Hand disappeared with billions in depositors' funds.

The CIA flirted with a similar operation in Hawaii, but eventually chose the Pakistan-based BCCI. It welcomed anyone with large amounts of cash to launder, provided by narcotics traffickers, arms merchants, terrorists and gangster governments.

Naturally, the CIA felt right at home. In fact, one former BCCI official claims to have been told that the CIA—and Director Richard Helms in particular—actually started the bank, and that it "wasn't a Pakistani bank at all."

Before collapsing, BCCI managed to facilitate a host of CIA covert operations, notably the first President Bush's efforts to pump weapons to Sadson's "unauthorized" arming of Libya (see Hit #30).

Efforts to unravel all of BCCI's mysteries will never succeed. Its directors had the good sense to feather the nests of enough prominent US politicians, of both parties, to ensure that any investigation would be halfhearted at best.

Not surprisingly, CIA-connected lobbyists worked to undermine any probe. Roughly $20 billion of BCCI's assets remain unaccounted for.

Hit #39: *Invading Panama*

For most of his life, Manuel Noriega got along very well with the CIA. As far back as 1959, he was reporting on Panamanian leftists to the Americans; by 1966, he was on the CIA payroll. Despite—or maybe because of—Noriega's "perverse" treatment of prisoners, he was deemed worthy to be trained at the notorious School of the Americas (more popularly known as "the School of Assassins"), run by the US Army in Panama City. (It's since moved to Ft. Benning, Georgia, and has been renamed WHINSEC.)

As early as 1972, reports of Noriega's drug trafficking reached the DEA, and the State Department complained of his dealings with other intelligence services, notably those of Israel and Cuba. *Don't worry,* the CIA told them, *he's our boy.*

In 1976, Noriega paid a visit to CIA Director George H. W. Bush in Washington. The new director was less comfortable with Noriega and took him off the CIA payroll, but when Bush became vice president in 1980, Noriega went back on, with a six-figure annual salary.

In 1981, Panama's popular head of state, Omar Torrijos, was killed in a plane crash; by 1983, Noriega had consolidated his control. In 1987, a close Noriega aide corroborated what many suspected—Noriega had sabotaged Torrijos' plane. (The CIA had also been linked to the assassination of Panama's president in 1955, allegedly with the approval of then-Vice-President Nixon).

Nothing Noriega did seemed to upset the CIA. If he smuggled cocaine on Contra supply planes (see Hits #22, #33 and #34) . . . well, he wasn't the only one. If he beheaded a political opponent who accused him of drug-running . . . well, he was just being firm. If he used violence and fraud to steal the 1984 Panamanian elections . . . well, we couldn't have been more pleased with the outcome.

By 1989, however, the love affair was over. Noriega had angered his handlers by waffling on opposing the Sandinistas in Nicaragua, and he was showing other disquieting signs of disobedience. In December 1989, US troops invaded Panama to "arrest" Noriega, slaughtering 2,000–4,000 innocent civilians in the process.

What changed after the invasion? Violence, fraud and drug trafficking continued unabated but, unlike Noriega, Panama's new rulers knew how to follow orders. Although the Canal reverted to their control in 1999, the US continued to operate in Panama through mercenaries and front companies. Lately we've negotiated a free-trade agreement, are building two new naval bases there, and have even been using Panama's airspace to test unmanned ("drone") aircraft.

Hit #40: *The First Iraq War*

The first Iraq War, in early 1991, didn't change much. Our old buddy, the despotic Emir of Kuwait, was placed back on his throne. Our former buddy, Saddam Hussein, while knocked down a peg or two, was still in power and as brutal as ever. Hundreds of thousands of Iraqis died, hundreds of US veterans were suffering from a mysterious disease, and the Persian Gulf was ravaged by the largest oil spill in history. The question naturally arises: Could any of this have been avoided?

The whole dispute started because Kuwait was slant drilling. Using equipment bought from National Security Council Chief Brent Scowcroft's old company, Santa Fe International, Kuwait was pumping out some $14 billion's worth of oil from underneath Iraqi territory. Even the territory they were drilling *from* had originally been Iraq's. Slant drilling can get you shot in Texas; in the Mideast, it was enough to start a war.

Even so, this dispute could have been negotiated. But it's hard to *avoid* a war when what you're actually doing is trying to *provoke* a war.

The most famous example of that was the meeting between Saddam and US Ambassador to Iraq April Glaspie, five days before Iraq invaded Kuwait. As CIA satellite photos showed an Iraqi invasion force massing on the Kuwaiti border, Glaspie told Hussein that "the US takes no position" on Iraq's dispute with Kuwait.

A few days later, during last-minute negotiations, Kuwait's foreign minister said: "We are not going to respond to [Iraq]. . . . If they don't like it, let them occupy our territory. . . . We are going to bring in the Americans." The US reportedly encouraged Kuwait's attitude.

Pitting the two countries against each other was nothing new. Back in 1989, CIA Director William Webster advised Kuwait's security chief to "take advantage of the deteriorating economic situation in Iraq . . . to put pressure on [it]." At the same time, a CIA-linked think tank was advising Saddam to put pressure on the Kuwaitis.

A month earlier, the administration of George H. W. Bush had issued a secret directive that called for greater economic cooperation with Iraq. This ultimately resulted in billions of dollars of illegal arms sales to Saddam.

The First Iraq War further destabilized the region and made Kuwait more dependent on us. It allowed US oil companies to exert more control over oil prices, and thus boost their profits. The US military got an excuse to build more bases in the region (which Saudi Arabia, for one, didn't want), and the war also helped justify the "need" to continue exorbitant levels of military spending. Finally, it sent a message to Third World leaders about what to expect if they dared step out of line.

Hit #41: **Destroying Haiti**

US troops invaded Haiti five times, once staying for almost twenty years (1915–34). At the end of that prolonged visit, during which we killed thousands of Haitians for daring to rebel, we left the country in the hands of the local National Guard, confident that they'd carry on our good work.

From this arrangement emerged the Duvalier family dynasty and their private terrorist force, the machete-wielding Tontons Macoutes. "Papa Doc" Duvalier (he was a medical doctor) also relied on voodoo incantations and, during a 1959 uprising, the timely assistance of the US military. When Papa Doc died in 1971, his nineteen-year-old son, called Baby Doc, became "president-for-life."

Throughout the blood-drenched rule of the Duvaliers (nearly 100,000 killed by the Tontons Macoutes alone), the US barely uttered a peep about human rights violations. In 1986, however, when it became apparent that Baby Doc's presidency could not in fact be sustained for his entire life (unless he died soon), the Reagan administration airlifted him to a retirement villa in France and started talking about the "democratic process."

Before that could begin, however, the Haitian military had to be further strengthened. CIA money began flowing to Haiti, which had already seen US aid double during the Reagan years. The CIA set up an antinarcotics service called—appropriately—SIN (the "national intelligence service"). As one CIA man admitted, SIN used its millions in CIA subsidies mainly to suppress popular movements by means of torture and assassination. Far from combatting drugs, many SIN officers engaged in the drug trade themselves.

In 1990, elections were finally allowed. Haitians stunned the US by rejecting the candidate we preferred in favor of a left-wing Catholic priest, Jean-Bertrand Aristide. The Bush administration could scarcely conceal its joy when Haiti's US-trained military deposed Aristide eight months later.

Bill Clinton negotiated his return to power in 1994, but Aristide had to step aside when his term ended sixteen months later—even though he had missed three years of it. Even this was too much for the CIA, which leaked a "psychological profile" that painted the courageous, dedicated Aristide as a "psychopath."

Aristide was overwhelmingly re-elected in 2000, but immediately faced violent opposition. With the covert backing of the George W. Bush administration, Aristide was forced back into exile in 2004, returning only after the devastating earthquake of 2011.

Given the longtime US support for drug traffickers, thugs and butchers within the Haitian military and police forces, the chances of a government coming to power that supports the needs of the Haitian people are slim to none.

Hit #42: *Dismembering Yugoslavia*

The bloodshed and chaos that engulfed Yugoslavia after its breakup have been portrayed as the inevitable result of bottled-up ethnic tensions. But there's considerable evidence that both the breakup and the warfare were encouraged by Western intelligence services—including Germany's BND, the successor to the Gehlen Org and their equivalent to the CIA (see Hit #1).

Germany's interests in the region date to World War II, when the Bosnians and Croats allied with the Nazis against the Serbs, who the Nazis regarded as *untermenschen* (subhumans). After Germany reunified in 1989, it began to take a more expansionist attitude toward Eastern Europe, and Yugoslavia in particular. In 1990, it urged the first Bush administration to help it dismantle Yugoslavia.

Bush was happy to comply, since the US had longstanding plans to overthrow Yugoslavia's government. Yugoslavia had recently renounced the market-oriented "shock treatment" prescribed for it (which had been causing social unrest), so it was a prime candidate for further destabilization.

The Germans encouraged Croatia to secede from Yugoslavia, and Bosnia soon followed. Germany immediately recognized the new nations, forcing the hand of the European Community, which had wanted to take a more cautious approach. The new Croatian state adopted the flag and anthem of its WWII Nazi puppet regime—and, in some cases, the same personnel.

Virulently fascist Croats had long been active in the World Anti-Communist League (see Hit #32) and other exile groups nurtured by the CIA. Many Eastern European Nazis had gone on to work with the CIA, either in the US or in covert operations abroad. With the collapse of Communism in Eastern Europe, many of these aging chickens came home to roost.

(Today, neofascist movements are gaining strength in many European countries, notably Austria, Belgium, and the Netherlands. Fueled by anti-immigrant and Islamophobic sentiments, the groups have been forging networks across Europe and abroad.)

Despite an official arms embargo against Croatia and Bosnia, Western powers immediately began covertly arming them, which would have been impossible without the knowledge and acquiescence of the CIA and the German BND. Mercenaries from Britain, Germany and the US served alongside the Croatian militias—a sure sign of an ongoing covert operation. In fact, in 1994, the CIA opened a new base in Albania to monitor troop movements and "potential targets" (see Hit #43).

Hit #43: *Kosovo and "The Snake"*

After the successful dismemberment of Yugo-slavia (see Hit #42), the CIA was ready for a repeat performance. With the help of a NATO bombing campaign, Kosovo was transformed from an impoverished semiautonomous province of Serbia with ongoing ethnic tensions into an impoverished semiautonomous UN protectorate with ongoing ethnic tensions. And as a special bonus, it ended up being run by an organized crime syndicate.

The role of "freedom fighters" in this scenario was played by the Kosovo Liberation Army, thuggish separatists organized with the help of the CIA and the German BND. The KLA were supplied with East German and Albanian weaponry, which they paid for mostly with proceeds from dealing drugs.

There was one possible impediment to this cozy arrangement—a popular nonviolent resistance movement dedicated to resolving tensions with Serbia through negotiation. That would mess everything up, so—to provoke a crisis—the KLA began attacking police stations and government offices in 1996.

By 1998 the crisis had escalated to the point of frequent skirmishes with Serbian forces. After one such battle near the village of Racak, the KLA dressed their dead in civilian clothes, fired extra bullets into them at close range, then stacked them in a ditch, claiming they were executed by Serbian forces. On hand to publicize this atrocity was William Walker, a veteran of US-backed warfare in Central America (like another William Walker 130 years earlier).

This helped take the conflict to the next level. "Negotiations" were held at Rambouillet, France, and the Serbs were given an ultimatum: surrender all of Yugoslavia to NATO occupation, or else. The Kosovars weren't represented by their elected president, the founder of the nonviolent

resistance; in his place was the 29-year-old commander of the KLA, Hashim "The Snake" Thaci. Not surprisingly, no agreement came out of this meeting.

After 78 days of bombing, what was left of Yugoslavia became even smaller, and NATO forces have been occupying Kosovo ever since. The whole operation was a field day for US companies. The public relations firm Ruder, Finn helped make the case for the war; mercenaries from MPRI, a private military contractor, helped with the training of KLA officers; Halliburton got to build Camp Bondsteel, the largest US military base constructed since the Vietnam War; and the CIA was able to establish a Guantanamo-like "secret" prison there, staffed by folks from the private US security firm DynCorp.

Hashim the Snake became prime minister of Kosovo where, according to investigators from the Council of Europe (an international human rights organization), he and his fellow KLA goons run a virtual mafia state that not only traffics in narcotics but also sex slaves and human organs. Perhaps it's time to renew that PR contract.

Hit #44: *The 9/11 Attacks*

As with the JFK assassination (see Hit #9), if the CIA had nothing to do with the 9/11 attacks, they have a peculiar way of showing it. The cochairs of the 9/11 Commission claimed the agency stonewalled them by withholding and destroying evidence, and the CIA's actions before, during and after the attacks give the overwhelming impression of an agency with something to hide.

Before 9/11, the paths of the nineteen alleged hijackers frequently crossed the CIA's—which isn't surprising, since the agency helped arm and train the mujahedeen in Afghanistan. Six of the hijackers were trained by a known CIA informant, and fifteen got their US visas through our consulate in Jeddah, Saudi Arabia, despite incomplete applications. A consular official there said he turned down many suspicious applicants, but was repeatedly overruled by CIA officers.

Although a number of the hijackers were under CIA surveillance as al-Qaeda operatives, they still managed to travel unmolested into and within the United States. Ziad Jarrah was detained and questioned in Dubai at the behest of the CIA, but was released without any blemish on his record that would have raised red flags when he was stopped for speeding in Maryland just two days before 9/11.

The German BND gave the CIA the US phone number of another future hijacker, but the CIA did nothing to track him down. Two others were monitored at a 9/11 planning meeting with Khalid Sheikh Mohammed in Malaysia—after which they moved to San Diego and shared an apartment with an FBI informant!

Alleged ringleader Mohamed Atta stands out as the Lee Harvey Oswald of 9/11—hanging out with intelligence agents and often seen in two places at once. Supposedly a devout Muslim, he lived with a stripper and loved alcohol, cocaine and pork chops.

Atta booked lessons at a flight school in Florida owned by Wally Hilliard, who got his planes from the same source as CIA drug smuggler Barry Seal, a stalwart of the Contra war. Although one of Hilliard's planes was caught with 43 tons of heroin, he was never charged.

Just prior to 9/11, suspicious stock transactions earned millions of dollars for a buyer with apparent foreknowledge of the attacks. Because of the attention, nobody claimed the money, but it was traced to a bank where CIA Executive Director "Buzzy" Krongard had previously been in charge. At the very hour of the attacks, future CIA Director Porter Goss was meeting with a Pakistani agent who'd authorized wiring $100,000 to Mohamed Atta.

The CIA's investigations of all these botched cases were so perfunctory that only minor reprimands were handed out, and most agents received no punishment at all.

Hit #45: *The Second Afghan War*

The CIA's destabilization of Afghanistan continued well after Soviet troops withdrew (see Hit #36). It supported a variety of fanatic Islamist groups, and when the Taliban, backed by Pakistan and Saudi Arabia, took power in 1996, the CIA smiled benignly on the new fundamentalist regime. The US hoped the Taliban would control enough of the country to negotiate new oil and gas pipelines.

But relations grew tense when Osama bin Laden returned to Afghanistan as the Taliban's guest. The wealthy heir of an influential Saudi family, bin Laden was a veteran of the CIA's massive Afghan war against the USSR. After the Soviet withdrawal, his al-Qaeda guerrillas backed insurgencies in Russia, China and Yugoslavia that seemed to be in line with US goals. But then he bombed US embassies in Africa, so when the Taliban welcomed him back to Afghanistan, the US soon imposed sanctions.

In 2001, however, hoping to renew the pipeline deal, George W. Bush's administration offered the Taliban $125 million in aid. (Laili Helms, the niece of former CIA Director Richard Helms, chaired the talks.) But when the Taliban insisted on seeing evidence before extraditing bin Laden (and when it became clear they were also pursuing a pipeline deal with Argentina), war plans were drawn up and presented to the president . . . on September 9, 2001.

After the 9/11 attacks two days later, those war plans were implemented, and US troops have been fighting in Afghanistan—and neighboring parts of Pakistan—ever since. The ostensible reason was to get bin Laden, but the real aim was to oust the Taliban and install a more pliable client regime. Bin Laden escaped across the border into Pakistan, with help from that country's double-dealing secret service, the ISI.

But who cared? A pipeline deal was signed within seven months of the US invasion. The new president, Hamid Karzai, had been a consultant for the Texas oil company Unocal—as had US Envoy, and later Ambassador, Zalmay Khalilzad. So Unocal basically negotiated with itself.

Meanwhile, the president's brother (Ahmed Wali Karzai, a longtime CIA asset who was assassinated in 2011) worked to reverse the Taliban's suppression of opium production. Thanks to his efforts, Afghanistan is once again the world's largest opium exporter. Even more impressive was its ranking, in 2010, as the second most corrupt nation on earth, tied with the brutal military dictatorship in Myanmar (i.e. Burma) and surpassed only by government-less Somalia.

The CIA and US troops are trying desperately to keep Karzai in power long enough to negotiate our withdrawal. The fondest desire of al-Qaeda leadership was that after 9/11, the US would invade Afghanistan and get bogged down there indefinitely. If so, mission accomplished.

Hit #46: *The Second Iraq War*

The CIA was blamed for providing "faulty intelligence" that lead to the second Iraq War, and it's true that the CIA was happy to tell the White House exactly what it wanted to hear. But in case that wasn't enough, old Team B veterans (see Hit #27), working under Dick Cheney, helped set up their own basement CIA to "stovepipe" real and manufactured intelligence to Cheney and thence to the media.

It was no secret that an invasion of Iraq was George W. Bush's top priority—even before he took the White House. Within hours of the 9/11 attacks, his administration was casting about for ways to blame Iraq, even though the CIA was tying it to al-Qaeda. "Sweep it all up," Donald Rumsfeld ordered. "Things related and not." The next day Bush, "testy and intimidating," was demanding a report on the connection between Iraq and 9/11.

Over the next eighteen months, Cheney paid eight visits to CIA headquarters, making sure they got things right. One veteran officer said, "Never have I seen [such] manipulation of intelligence." Others within the CIA tried to provide an accurate picture of Iraq's capabilities—that it had no "weapons of mass destruction." The White House would have none of it, hinting darkly about nebulous al-Qaeda ties and possible "mushroom clouds" until they got their invasion.

But just to make sure, Rumsfeld set up the Office of Special Plans. The OSP was given access to raw intelligence, which it interpreted to suit the views of its patrons. One officer called the OSP "aberrant, pervasive and contrary to good order and discipline," and charged that it not only cooked the books on the case for war, but blithely ignored the obvious difficulties that an occupation of Iraq would entail.

Many Iraqi defectors were happy to manufacture stories about Iraq's nonexistent WMDs. The German BND, believed—correctly—that one source, code-named "Curveball," was lying, but his stories were still used as the backbone of the case for war.

In the end, CIA Director George Tenet stood behind Secretary of State Colin Powell (literally) as he presented these half-truths and distortions to the UN. And once the war began, the CIA functioned virtually as a fifth branch of the military—running interrogations, hiring subcontractors and mounting "special operations."

Ironically, a 2006 National Intelligence Estimate (which reports the consensus of a dozen different intelligence agencies) found that invading and occupying Iraq had "helped spawn a new generation of Islamic radicalism and that the overall terrorist threat has grown."

Hit #47: *The Valerie Plame Scandal*

The CIA's status diminished during the George W. Bush years. As of 2005, it was no longer a *Central* Intelligence Agency that oversaw the others; instead, it became one of sixteen intelligence agencies that reported to the new Director of National Intelligence (four others remained under the control of the Pentagon). This reflected the White House's desire to be able to go "spy shopping" to get reports it needed to support its policies (see Hit #46).

The Valerie Plame scandal is symbolic of the CIA's demotion, as political operatives in the White House deliberately blew the cover of a covert CIA officer. They did that to get revenge against Plame's husband, Ambassador Joseph Wilson, who'd embarrassed the White House by publicly contradicting one of the contrived bits of "intelligence" it produced to show that Saddam's Iraq was on the verge of acquiring nuclear weapons.

The White House had asked the CIA to look into cables, obtained from the Italian spy agency SISMI, that alleged Iraq was attempting to illegally import highly enriched uranium from Niger. Since Wilson had been posted to both Iraq and Niger as a diplomat, and was familiar with officials in both countries, the CIA picked him to investigate. It didn't take him long to determine that the Italian cables were forgeries, and crude ones at that.

Wilson told the CIA that there was nothing to the allegations and considered the matter closed. So he was both dismayed and amazed when President Bush included the phony "evidence" in his 2003 State of the Union address. Wilson published an op-ed in *The New York*

Times a few months later that said, "I have little choice but to conclude that some of the intelligence related to Iraq's nuclear weapons program was twisted to exaggerate the Iraqi threat."

Although justifications for the Second Iraq War were by then moot (since the war had already started), the White House went ballistic. It launched a smear campaign against Wilson that insinuated that he had only been picked to investigate because "his wife, Valerie Plame . . . an agency operative" had suggested him. This blew the cover not just of Plame but of everyone she worked with.

(And what was Plame's job at the CIA? Working to prevent the proliferation of weapons of mass destruction.)

Years later, an investigation by the Italian parliament fingered several ex-CIA agents close to the White House as the likely source of the forged documents. This suggests that the reason Bush's cronies freaked out over Wilson's article was that it pointed toward a very uncomfortable truth: Beyond just shopping around for bad intelligence, they seem to have also had a hand in creating it.

Hit #48: *"Enhanced Interrogation"*

After 9/11, Dick Cheney let the country know that we would be working on "the dark side. . . . We've got to spend time in the shadows in the intelligence world . . . without any discussion."

To that end, the White House commissioned a legal finding that allowed the CIA to use specific illegal torture methods. These methods filtered down into the military and were used against thousands of detainees, many of whom had been swept up by bounty hunters or people who simply wanted to even scores. Most were completely innocent, and they included the mentally ill, children as young as thirteen, and an 89-year-old man suffering from dementia.

Under torture, many of these prisoners confessed to all sorts of imaginary crimes, sending US forces out on wild goose chases. One innocent man, a health club manager from Kuwait, was tortured for months to make him keep repeating his initial lies.

A presumed al-Qaeda leader was waterboarded 187 times in a single month and still failed to produce any useful intelligence. As veteran interrogators have long known, nonviolent methods lead to much better information. But, in many cases, false confessions were what interrogators wanted to hear—to build the case for war in Iraq (see Hit #46).

The world learned of these "enhanced interrogation" methods when gruesome photos were published from Saddam's torture chambers at Abu Ghraib prison, reopened under US management—a huge recruiting boost for Islamist radicals. The CIA also ran interrogations at the US base in Guantanamo, Cuba, and at dozens of other "black sites" around the world.

Detainees were stripped, shaved, shackled and hooded, then subjected to stress positions, sleep deprivation, water torture, mock executions, rape and sexual humiliation. According to White House lawyer John Yoo, the president has the right to have a child's testicles crushed if he thinks doing that will extract useful information from the boy's parents.

If that wasn't enough, the CIA used "extraordinary rendition," under which suspects were kidnapped and sent to countries like Egypt, Syria, Pakistan, Morocco, Jordan, and Libya, where there were no restraints on the use of torture. CIA agents stood by and supplied the questions, while others did the torturing.

To their credit, there were people in the White House, the CIA and the military who opposed these methods, but they were overruled. More than a hundred detainees died while in US custody; some were beaten or tortured to death, others commited suicide. The day before General David Petraeus took over as CIA director, prosecutors announced they were dropping their investigations against the agency in 99 such deaths, leaving just two cases open.

Sources

I relied on two sources more than others: William Blum's indispensible overview *The CIA: A Forgotten History* (Zed Books, 1986; reissued as *Killing Hope* in 1995 by Common Courage Press), referred to below simply as *Blum;* and the now-defunct periodical *Covert Action Information Bulletin,* referred to below as *CAIB.* For lots of additional web links (plus everything that's listed here), go to ***http://tinyurl.com/CIAsources***.   *Mark Zepezauer*

Introduction: Noam Chomsky, *How the World Works*, Soft Skull Press, 2011, p. 162. **Hit #1:** E.H. Cookridge, *Gehlen: Spy of the Century*, Random House, 1971; Carl Oglesby, "The Secret Treaty of Fort Hunt," *CAIB* #35 (Fall 1990); Charles Higham, *Trading With the Enemy*, Delacorte, 1983; Ladislas Farago, *Aftermath*, Avon, 1974. **Hit #2:** Warren Hinckle, "The CIA's 'secret army' activity in Italy," *San Francisco Examiner*, 11/22/90; Patrice Claude, "Strange tale of terrorism, sabotage shakes Italy," *San Francisco Chronicle*, 11/14/90; William Scobie, "Secret army's war on the left," *London Observer*, 11/18/90. **Hit #3:** Blum, Ch. 9; National Security Archive, **Hit #4:** Stephen Kinzer, *Bitter Fruit: The Untold Story of the American Coup in Guatemala*, Anchor, 1983; Blum, Ch. 10. **Hit #5:** Walter Bowart, *Operation Mind Control*, Dell, 1978; John Marks, *The Search for the Manchurian Candidate*, Dell, 1979. **Hit #6:** Blum, Ch. 26 & 42. **Hit #7:** Michael Beschloss, *Mayday: Eisenhower, Khrushchev and the U-2 Affair*, Harper & Row, 1986; Fletcher Prouty, *JFK: The CIA, Vietnam and the Plot to Assassinate John F. Kennedy*, Birch Lane, 1992. **Hit #8:** Warren Hinckle & William Turner, *Deadly Secrets: The CIA-Mafia War Against Castro and the Assassination of JFK*, Thunder's Mouth, 1992; Blum, Ch. 30. **Hit #9:** Philip Melanson, *Spy Saga: Lee Harvey Oswald and US Intelligence*, Praeger, 1990; Jim Marrs, *Crossfire: The Plot That Killed Kennedy*, Carroll & Graf, 1989. **Hit #10:** Marilyn B. Young, *The Vietnam Wars 1945–1990*, Harper Perennial, 1991. **Hit #11:** Blum, Ch. 29. **Hit #12:** Karl Evanzz, *The Judas Factor: The Plot to Kill Malcolm X*, Thunder's Mouth, 1992. **Hit #13:** Blum, Ch. 14 & 31. **Hit #14:** Blum, Ch. 3 & 35. **Hit #15:** Philip Melanson, *Who Killed Martin Luther King?*, Odonian, 1993; *CAIB* #34 (Summer 1990). **Hit #16:** Philip Melanson, *Who Killed Robert Kennedy?*, Odonian, 1993; William Turner & Jonn Christian, *The Assassination of Robert F. Kennedy*, Thunder's Mouth, 1993; Robert Morrow, *The Senator Must Die,*

Roundtable, 1988. **Hit #17:** Blum, Ch. 34**. Hit #18:** Young (see Hit #10); Blum, Ch. 19. **Hit #19:** William Shawcross, *Sideshow: Nixon, Kissinger and the Destruction of Cambodia*, Simon and Schuster, 1979; Blum, Ch. 20. **Hit #20:** Blum, Ch. 21. **Hit #21:** Verne Lyon, "The History of Operation CHAOS," *CAIB* #34 (Summer 1990). **Hit #22:** Alfred McCoy, *The Politics of Heroin in Southeast Asia*, Harper Colophon, 1973; Peter Dale Scott & Jonathan Marshall, *Cocaine Politics*, University of California, 1992. **Hit #23:** Jim Hougan, *Secret Agenda: Watergate, Deep Throat and the CIA*, Random House, 1984; Deborah Davis, *Katherine the Great: Katherine Graham and* The Washington Post, Harcourt Brace Jovanovitch, 1979; Len Colodny & Robert Gettelin, *Silent Coup: The Removal of a President*, St. Martins, 1991. **Hit #24:** Carl Bernstein, "The CIA and the Media," *Rolling Stone*, 10/20/77. **Hit #25:** John Stockwell, *In Search of Enemies*, Norton, 1978; Blum, Ch. 41. **Hit #26:** Donald Freed & Fred Landis, *Death in Washington: The Murder of Orlando Letelier*, Laurence Hill, 1980. **Hit #27:** Mark Perry, *The Last Days of the CIA*, William Morrow, 1992. **Hit #28:** John Judge, "The Black Hole of Guyana" in *Secret and Suppressed*, edited by Jim Keith, Feral House, 1993. **Hit #29:** Barbara Honneger, *October Surprise*, Tudor, 1989; Robert Parry, *Trick or Treason*, Sheridan Square, 1993. **Hit #30:** Jack Anderson, *Fiasco*, Times Books, 1983; John M. Blair, *The Control of Oil*, Vintage Books, 1976; Peter Maas, *Manhunt*, Random House, 1986. George Tremlett, *Gadaffi: The Desert Mystic*, Carroll & Graf, 1993. **Hit #31:** Ellen Ray & Bill Schaap, "US Crushes Caribbean Jewel," *CAIB* #20 (Winter 1984); Blum, Ch. 45. **Hit #32:** Blum, Ch. 48; Scott & Jon Lee Anderson, *Inside the League*, Dodd, Mead, 1986. Raymond Bonner, *Weakness and Deceit*, Times Books, 1984. **Hit #33:** Peter Kornbluh, *Nicaragua: The Price of Intervention*, IPS, 1987; Leslie Cockburn, *Out of Control*, Atlantic Monthly Press, 1987. **Hit #34:** Theodore Draper, *A Very Thin Line*, Hill and Wang, 1991; Doug Vaughn, "Walsh's Final Iran-Contra Report," *CAIB* #48 (Spring 1994). **Hit #35:** Maggie Mahar, "Unwitting Accomplices?" *Barrons*, 12/17/90; Roy Rowan, "Pan Am 103: Why Did They Die?" *Time*, 4/27/92; Jeff Jones, "The Bombing of Pan Am 103," *CAIB* #34 (Summer 1990). **Hit #36:** "Under the Bush with the CIA" (John Stockwell interview), *Z Magazine*, September 1989. **Hit #37:** Glen Alcalay, "Bombed, robbed, relocated, irradiated by US, France," *National Guardian* (US), 11/25/87; *CAIB* #29 (Winter 1988). **Hit #38:** Jonathan Kwitny, *The Crimes of Patriots*, Touchstone Books, 1988;

Mark Potts, *Dirty Money: The World's Sleaziest Bank*, National Press, 1992; Jack Calhoun, "BCCI: Bank of the CIA," *CAIB* #44 (Spring 1993); "The BCCI-CIA Connection: How Far Did It Go?", *Newsweek*, 12/7/92. **Hit #39:** Independent Commission of Inquiry on the US Invasion of Panama, *The US Invasion of Panama: The Truth behind Operation "Just Cause,"* South End, 1991. **Hit #40:** Ramsey Clark, *The Fire This Time: US War Crimes in the Gulf,* Thunder's Mouth, 1992. **Hit #41:** John Canham-Clyde, "Haiti: Selling Out Democracy," *CAIB* #48 (Spring 1994). **Hit #42:** Sean Gervasi, "Germany, US and the Yugoslavia Crisis," *CAIB* #43 (Winter 1992–93). **Hit #43:** David Gibbs, *First Do No Harm: Humanitarian Intervention and the Destruction of Yugoslavia,* Vanderbilt University Press, 2009. **Hit #44:** Thomas Kean and Lee Hamilton, "Stonewalled by the CIA," *The New York Times,* 1/2/08; James Risen and Eric Lichtblau, "C.I.A. Was Given Data On Hijacker Long Before 9/11," *The New York Times,* 2/4/04; Seth Ackerman, "Who Knew? The Unanswered Questions of 9/11," *In These Times,* 9/4/03; Daniel Hopsicker, *Welcome to Terrorland: Mohamed Atta & the 9/11 Cover-up in Florida,* Trine Day Books, 2004; "India helped FBI trace ISI-terrorist links," *Times of India,* 10/9/01. **Hit #45:** Ahmed Rashid, *Taliban: Militant Islam, Oil and Fundamentalism in Central Asia,* Second Edition, Yale University Press, 2010; Seymour Hersh, "The Getaway," *The New Yorker,* 1/28/02; Alfred W. McCoy, "The Opium Wars in Afghanistan: Can Anyone Pacify the World's Number One Narco-State?" *Asia-Pacific Journal,* 3/30/10. **Hit #46:** Thomas E. Ricks, *Fiasco, The American Military Adventure in Iraq,* Penguin Press, 2006; Joel Roberts, "Plans For Iraq Attack Began On 9/11," CBS News, 9/10/09; Mark Mazzetti, "Spy Agencies Say Iraq War Worsens Terrorism Threat," *The New York Times,* 9/24/06. **Hit #47:** Valerie Plame Wilson, *Fair Game: My Life as a Spy, My Betrayal by the White House,* Simon & Schuster, 2007; Joseph Wilson, *The Politics of Truth: A Diplomat's Memoir: Inside the Lies that Led to War and Betrayed My Wife's CIA Identity,* Public Affairs, 2005. **Hit #48:** Jason Leopold, "CIA Watchdog Report Says Detainees Died During Interrogations," *The Public Record,* 4/20/09; R. Jeffrey Smith, "Hill Panel Reviewing CIA Tactics," *The Washington Post,* 5/10/09; Nat Hentoff, "Cheney's 'Dark Arts,'" *The Village Voice,* 11/8/05; David Leigh, James Ball, Ian Cobain and Jason Burke, "Guantanamo Files: Massive Leak Reveals Innocent Detainees," *The Guardian* (UK), 4/24/11.

Index

OTHER REAL STORY BOOKS

HOW THE WORLD WORKS   NOAM CHOMSKY

Noam Chomsky has long been the most cited living author; on the all-time list, he's eighth (after Marx, Lenin, Shakespeare, Aristotle, the Bible, Plato and Freud). Lionized abroad, he's by far the most important social critic in the world, but his political ideas are marginalized in the US.

The material collected here was originally published in four short books that together sold 593,000 copies. Made up of intensively edited speeches and interviews, this book offers something that's not easy to find—pure Chomsky, with every dazzling idea and penetrating insight intact, delivered in clear, accessible, reader-friendly prose.   *336 pp. • $18*

9/11: THE SIMPLE FACTS
WHY THE OFFICIAL STORY CAN'T POSSIBLY BE TRUE
ARTHUR NAIMAN ET AL.

Books on 9/11 tend to get dismissed as "conspiracy theories" but that won't work with this one, because it contains *no theories at all* about who did what. It simply focuses on flaws in the official version of what happened—flaws that have led more than 1,650 architects and engineers, with more than 25,000 years of combined professional experience, to demand a new, independent investigation.

It begins by discussing fourteen clearly observable facts about the collapse of the World Trade Center buildings that the official story can't explain, then gives a simple explanation that accounts for all of them. It goes on to examine many other questionable aspects of what happened on 9/11.

The sorts of questions it raises (and there are hundreds of them) have convinced not just building professionals but tens of thousands of others—senior government, intelligence, military and law enforcement officials, pilots, firefighters, 9/11 survivors and relatives, scholars, etc.— that we need a new investigation. Read this book and you'll end up agreeing with them.   *112 pp. • $12*

Printed in the United States
by Baker & Taylor Publisher Services